NO MOUNTAIN
HIGH ENOUGH

NO MOUNTAIN HIGH ENOUGH

Secrets of Successful
African American Women

DOROTHY EHRHART-MORRISON, PH.D.

CONARI PRESS
Berkeley, CA

Conari Press books are distributed by Publishers Group West

ISBN: 0-943233-98-4

Cover design by Suzanne Albertson
Cover collage by Cynthia Goldstone
Author photo by Vogue Photography, Santa Monica, CA

Library of Congress Cataloging-in-Publication Data
Ehrhart-Morrison, Dorothy, 1930–
No mountain high enough: secrets of successful African American women /
Dorothy Ehrhart-Morrison.
p. cm.
Includes bibliographical references and index.
ISBN 0-943233-98-4 (alk. paper)
1. Afro-American women executives—Biography.
2. Afro-American women in the professions—Biography.
I. Title.
HD6054.4.U6E36   1997
646.7'0082—dc20   96-44167

This book

is dedicated to

my husband Saul Morrison,

my daughter Donna Key,

my granddaughters

Allegra Hayes and Lauren Key,

and my granddaughters by marriage

Kisha Key and Gabriella Leone.

ACKNOWLEDGMENTS

Every book including this one is a collaborative effort. Without the support and encouragement of many people, it would have remained a dream.

I want to thank Ethel Parker for her editorial assistance while the manuscript was in its infancy. Sincere thanks to my literary agent, Janell Walden-Agyeman. Janell you "believed." The expertise and the warm friendship of my editor, Barbara Quick, was invaluable. Much thanks, Barbara.

I wish to extend my heartfelt appreciation for the encouragement of "two Marys." Mary Poplin, my professor at Claremont Graduate School who planted the seed—she knew a book like this was needed. And, my Conari Press executive editor, Mary Jane Ryan, who helped cultivate that seed to its fruition. Mary Jane gave this greenhorn writer not only an opportunity to write, but had the patience, insight, and TLC to guide me along the way. Mary Jane, thanks for helping me unveil the hidden spirit of this work.

I want to thank my family and close friends who have encouraged me from beginning to end. I especially thank my husband, Saul, who kept the house going, while I kept the computer going; my daughter, Donna Key, bless you for being you; my sister-in-law June Zuckerman, supporter extraordinaire, Dr. Dorris Woods, my friend and college colleague; Prissy McClendon, my sister; and my friends Peggy Patterson, Lynne Emile, Annette Shamey, Ariann Swinson, Almeta Washington, and Dr. Michelle Wittig, who were my main cheerleaders.

Most of all, I want to thank the thirty-two women who so graciously allowed me to enter their lives and stay awhile.

CONTENTS

FOREWORD

WE HAVE WAITED A LONG TIME for a book like *No Mountain High Enough*. This book shows that African American women can and do flourish in high-status careers. The women profiled here have shown by their success and contributions to society that civil rights activists like Martin Luther King, Jr. and my husband, Medgar Evers, and others who fought and died for equal opportunities for all, did not die in vain.

Like my own life, the lives of these women were strengthened as they moved through considerable obstacles to triumph. Despite these obstacles, they were able, with clarity and life-affirming vision, to crystallize their values, needs, and dreams into realizable career goals.

Similar and distinctive elements in the struggle toward personal goals marked each woman's climb to the top: high intelligence, morality, values and ethics, education, personal commitment to careers, persistence, ability, some luck, and self-confidence. In addition, each woman's life was enriched by role models, mentors, spiritual guidance, and support from family members, extended family, colleagues, and friends. Each had a profound love for what she did, and gave back to the community and the country what had been given to her.

Myrlie Evers-Williams
Chairman, NAACP

INTRODUCTION

MORE THAN 20 YEARS after the assassination of Dr. Martin Luther King, Jr., many people wonder what has happened to his dream, and to black people in the United States of America. If someone from another country were to learn about the black American community based on the sensational reports of newspapers, magazines, radio, and television, he or she would see a depraved racial subgroup of gang-bangers, drug addicts, shiftless welfare recipients, and mean-spirited participants in domestic violence, hovered over by a constellation of a dozen or so world-famous and very glamorous athletes and Hollywood stars. Most white people in this country, bombarded by such images, know next to nothing about the flip side of the coin—about the black Americans who are quietly making monumental social, political, economic, and educational contributions to this country, who are working every day to make Dr. King's dream of racial equality, equal opportunity, and human dignity become a reality.

This book is about thirty-two women among the thousands of black Americans today whose lives could serve as a model to any person in this country, of any color. What combination of factors conspired to make these women so extraordinarily successful, often despite tremendous odds? There were no miracles involved: All of these women have worked hard in their lives to get to where they are now. And all of them had the love and support of parents and grandparents who made even greater

1

sacrifices, and beat even greater odds, in paving the way for their childrens' success. Again and again in these women's stories, you'll hear the theme of family values that fostered self-esteem, ambition, honor, and a sense of responsibility. These women grew up believing that the sky was the limit, and as a consequence they have scaled great heights.

They are not alone. Although they have faced daunting obstacles over the years, more black Americans are living productive and successful lives and filling leadership roles throughout the country than ever before. Voters are sending black representatives to Congress, and electing black mayors, in increasing numbers. In 1993, for the first time in history, a black woman was elected to the United States Senate. We have black state senators, assemblymembers, and judges, black women entrepreneurs, college presidents, architects, builders and developers, rocket scientists, bankers, mathematicians, physicians, philanthropists, psychiatrists, pathologists, lawyers, dentists, college professors, ministers, veterinarians, corporate executive officers, and epidemiologists.

This was not always the case. In the '40s and '50s, when I was growing up, most black parents who sacrificed to send their daughter to college did not look beyond the hope and possibility of their child's becoming a teacher. Getting a "Mrs." degree from a good man who had a good job was just as prized. Successful careers were not something black families in general dwelled on: Education was not considered a stepping-stone to high corporate positions or political office. Success was measured in simpler terms—you were successful if you had a job, if you were married, if you could feed your family, if you had a roof over your head, if you could educate your children.

About the time I graduated from college, in 1951, black women were slowly entering jobs and professions that had previously been closed to them. Banks were hiring black women as tellers, telephone companies were hiring them as operators, and they were being hired in civil service jobs. It took the civil rights movement of the '60s, the women's movement of the '70s, affirmative action, and the toil of many tenacious and idealistic individuals to advance the cause of fair and equal employment in all arenas of American life.

And yet when I proposed writing about black women in high-status careers for my Ph.D. dissertation, I was asked by a faculty member, "*Are there any black women in high-status careers?*" This was in 1988. I ended up researching and writing my dissertation, uncovering the extent to which the careers of successful black women (apart from black women entertainers) have not only been invisible in the media, but have also been ignored completely by the social scientists of our day. Millions of dollars are spent, and extensive data is collected, in attempts to find solutions to the problems of the black underclass in America. I was interested in the possibility that solutions to poverty could be found by researching the lives of black Americans who have succeeded rather than by focussing exclusively on those who have failed. Success leaves clues. If those clues can be articulated, perhaps we can find a way to teach success in our society—to make success a matter of equal opportunity.

At this time in our history when many of the people in power would have us return to an era of limited opportunities for people of color and limited freedoms for women, it seems especially important to present a fair and clear portrait of what it means to be black, female, and successful in this nation. I've written this book not to show that everything's rosy now for black women in the United States—because this is not at all the case. The thirty-two women profiled here are the exception rather than the rule: They are not only exceptionally bright and talented, but exceptionally tenacious as well. They have a great deal to say to the rest of America about what it takes to make personal dreams come true, to beat the odds, to rise to the top, to vault over the double hurdles of racism and sexism. Their achievements and their tenacity should be an inspiration to all in this country—especially to young black women—who aspire to do great things with their lives and a message to those people who harbor a belief that there is no ambition, nobility of purpose, or singularity of vision in the black community. The stories these women have to tell will lay all such beliefs to rest.

To make this book easier to read and understand, I've provided thumbnail sketches of the thirty-two women whose voices and life stories are interwoven throughout the text.

DONZALEIGH ABERNATHY Stage, screen, and television actor Donzaleigh Abernathy is the child of civil rights movement leader Ralph Abernathy. Her movie and television credits include *The Long Walk Home, Night of the Running Man, Ned Blessing, Amazing Grace* and *Homestead*, soon to be released on PBS. Divorced, Abernathy has no children.

BRENDA BASS, M.D. A pediatrician in Beverly Hills, California, Bass is married to a vice president of a prestigious investment brokerage firm. She is the parent of a daughter, seven years old, and a son who is four.

VIVIAN BOWSER The past president of the Texas Teachers Association, Vivian Bowser taught biology and science for many years in the Houston public schools. A widow, she had no children. Ms. Bowser passed away November 5, 1995.

ALETA CARPENTER Before recently founding her own resource development company, Carpenter worked for many years in radio, rising from unpaid intern to news announcer, news and public affairs director, religious director, station manager and president at an Oakland, California, radio station. She is married to a bacteriologist and has a son and a daughter.

JEWEL PLUMMER COBB, PH.D. The first African American to be appointed president of the California State University, Fullerton, Cobb holds a master of science degree and a doctorate in cell physiology from New York University. Before her appointment to California State University, Fullerton, Cobb held deanships at Douglass College at Rutgers and Connecticut College and several teaching positions, including tenured professor in the biology department at Sarah Lawrence College, Bronxville, New York. The recipient of several honorary doctorates, Cobb is divorced.

PAT COWINGS, PH.D. A principal investigator at the Psycho-Physiological Research Laboratory at Ames Research Center, NASA, Cowings was the first American woman to receive Scientist Astronaut Training (two years) as part of a NASA Shuttle Simulation Program. She is married to a co-investigator and has a nine-year-old son.

HENRIETTA DAVIS-BLACKMON Concert singer Henrietta Davis-Blackmon's operatic roles include Carmen in *Carmen Jones,* Clara in *Porgy and Bess,* Linda in *Lost in the Stars,* Fiordiligi in *Cosi fan Tutte,* Countess in *La Nozze di Figaro,* Zerlina in *Don Giovanni,* and Musetta in *La Bohème.* She is married and has no children.

ELOISE GREENFIELD Eloise Greenfield is the author of more than twenty children's books. Her special achievement awards include: The Carter G. Woodson Book Award for her biography, *Rosa Parks,* the New York Times Outstanding Book Award, the Irma Simonton Black Book Award, the Jane Addams Children's Book Award, the Coretta Scott King Award, the National Black Child Development Instructors, and the Washington D.C. Mayor's Art Award for Literature. Married, she is the mother of a son and a daughter.

KAYCEE HALE Kaycee Hale is founder and executive director of the Resource and Research Center, the world's largest network of educationally affiliated fashion research centers. Previously she worked as a fashion model; a librarian for the City of Los Angeles; a faculty member at Los Angeles Trade Technical College; president of the Fashion Company, Los Angeles; and co-host of a television show called *The Fashion Game*. A widow with no children, Hale is a renowned inspirational speaker with a schedule that takes her all over the world.

D. ANTOINETTE HANDY A retired Director of Music of The National Endowment of the Arts, Handy has performed as soloist, recitalist, symphony orchestra member, and recording artist, and is a lecturer and music consultant. Before going to the Endowment, she held university professorships at Tuskegee Institute and Virginia State University. Married and recently retired, she has three children.

MARY JANE HEWITT, PH.D. In addition to heading her own company, Samjai Fine Arts, Inc., Hewitt is associate editor of The International Review of African American Art, a quarterly publication that features visual arts of people of African descent. Previously, she served as the director of the Museum of African American Art in Los Angeles. Hewitt is married to a retired businessman. They have no children.

LEONTINE T. C. KELLY Leontine Turpeau Current Kelly is the first African American woman to be elected Bishop in the United Methodist Church. She was pastor at Galilee United Methodist church in Edwardville, Virginia and at Asbery Church in Richmond, Virginia, before moving to national headquarters in Nashville, Tennessee, to be in charge of evangelism. A widow and the mother of four children, Kelly continues to preach as a visiting professor at seminaries and at religious gatherings.

JENNIFER LAWSON At the time of the interviews, Jennifer Lawson was vice president for programming and promotional services at PBS. Honored as one of the 101 Most Influential People in the *Entertainment Today–Entertainment Weekly* Magazine, Lawson has served on panels to choose recipients of grants from the National Endowment of the Arts. Married to a businessman, she has two sons.

HARRIET RICHARDSON MICHEL Michel heads the National Minority Supplier Development Council, a twenty-five-year-old minority business institute. Her career profile includes special projects director, National Scholarship Service and Funds for Black Students; assistant, Office of the Mayor of New York; director of youth employment, U.S. Department of Labor, Washington, D.C.; consultant, Department of Housing and Development, Washington, D.C.; and president, New York City Urban League. Married for more than twenty-five years to a businessman, she is the mother of two sons.

REVEREND ELLA PEARSON MITCHELL, D.M. Mitchell is the director of continuing education and associate professor of Christian education at the School of Theology, Virginia Union University. Her books include *Those Preachin' Women* and *Women: to Preach or Not to Preach.* She has been married to a Baptist minister for almost fifty years and is the mother of four children.

EILEEN NORTON Norton is vice president of the Norton Family Foundation, a grant-giving institution that funds cultural and humanitarian projects. In 1993 Norton founded the Forum on Children's Issues, and she currently serves on the boards of the Children's Defense Fund, the New Museum of Contemporary Art, and the Hollywood Policy Center. She and her husband are the parents of two young children.

CYNTHIA SHEPARD PERRY, PH.D. U.S. Ambassador (Ret.) Cynthia Perry served her country as ambassador to two African countries, Sierra Leone and Burundi. Perry has also served as a dean of Peace Corps, Kenya; a staff development officer, U.N. Economic Commission, Addis Ababa, Ethiopia; a professor of education, Texas Southern University, and chief education and human resources officer, AID, Washington, D.C. She is married to a university professor and is the mother of four children.

LYDIA PETTIS-PATTON, PH.D Director of Leisure Services in Portsmouth, Virginia, Pettis-Patton has overall responsibility for the recreation and parks department, and the city's museums, libraries, and golf courses, as well as the bureau of convention centers and tourism. She is married to a university professor; they have a teenage son and daughter.

VIVIAN W. PINN, M.D. Pinn is the assistant director of The National Institutes of Health on Women's Health, and director of The Office of Research on Women's Health. Previously she was professor and chairman of pathology at Howard University. In July 1989, Pinn became the National Medical Association's eighty-eighth president, the second woman in its history to hold the position. Named as one of the one hundred most influential African Americans by *Ebony* magazine, she is divorced and has no children.

DOLORES RATCLIFFE Ratcliffe is president and CEO of Corita Communications, Inc., a market research, training, and consulting firm. She is the author of five books, and is often invited to speak on national and international issues pertaining to entrepreneurship, leadership, team building, time management, and networking through self-marketing. She is married to a retired university dean of engineering and computer science; they have no children.

IRIS RIDEAU Rideau is president of Rideau and Associates where she directs a staff of twenty-six workers in sales, administration, and marketing. She is separated and has one daughter from a previous marriage.

BETYE SAAR Artist Betye Saar's work is found in many galleries and museums throughout the world, including the Hirshhorn Museum and Gardens in Washington, D.C.; the Oakland Museum in Oakland, California; the New Jersey State Museum in Newark; the Philadelphia Academy of Fine Arts and the Philadelphia Museum of Art; the San Francisco Museum of Modern Art; the Museum of Fine Arts in Boston; and the Afro-American Museum in Los Angeles. Divorced, she is the mother of three daughters.

NORMA SKLAREK The first African American woman to receive a license to practice architecture in the United States, Sklarek's architectural credits include the city hall at San Bernardino, California, Terminal One at the Los Angeles International Airport, the Los Angeles Pacific Design Center, the United States embassy in Tokyo, the Fox Hills Mall in Culver City, California, and the South Coast Plaza in Orange County, California. Sklarek is married to a physician and is the mother of two sons.

ZELMA STENNIS Zelma Stennis heads one of the few important African American family-owned restaurant chains in the United States, the Golden Bird Restaurants, which has twelve locations. An active member of the Los Angeles community, she was selected by Mayor Tom Bradley to become the first African American to serve on the Los Angeles Convention and Tourism Commission. Married for more than 40 years before her husband's death in 1993, she raised four sons.

JACKIE TATUM Tatum is general manager of the Los Angeles Recreation and Parks Department and the first African American to head the nearly one-hundred-year-old department. She has the responsibility for the jobs of more than 2,000 workers and a 96 million dollar budget. Married for nearly twenty years, she is divorced and the mother of a son and a daughter.

SUSAN L. TAYLOR As editor-in-chief of *Essence* magazine, Taylor has been responsible for guiding the magazine through a period of phenomenal growth. Her popular column, "In The Spirit," which appears monthly in the magazine, has been the foundation of two popular books. In addition, for more than four seasons, Taylor was host and executive producer of *Essence,* the country's first nationally syndicated black-oriented television magazine show. Taylor is married and is the mother of a daughter.

BARBARA THEARD Barbara Theard is assistant vice president and a branch manager for the Bank of America. A divorced single mother, Theard is planning an imminent retirement, with thoughts of returning to college full-time.

DORIS TOPSY-ELVORD Doris Topsy-Elvord is a member of the city council in Long Beach, California. For most of her career, she worked as a youth authority counselor, a procurement officer, and a deputy probation officer–consultant. In 1991, she was honored by the U.S. Congress as a "Pioneer of Distinction" and published in the Congressional Library of Congress. Married, Topsy-Elvord is the mother of three sons.

FAYE WASHINGTON Washington is the assistant general manager for the Los Angeles Water and Power Department, one of the largest and most financially powerful organizations in the country. An inspirational speaker at conferences and meetings, she supports personal development programs and has spent many hours organizing motivational seminars for workers interested in career advancement. Married to a police detective, she is the mother of two teenage daughters.

RUTH WASHINGTON Ruth Washington was, for many years, the president and publisher of the *Los Angeles Sentinel* Newspaper, one of the premiere African American newspapers in the country. She passed away a few months after being interviewed for this book. She was seventy-six years old.

DIANE EDITH WATSON, PH.D. Diane Watson is a California State senator. A former member of the Los Angeles Board of Education, she is president of the National Organization of Black Elected Legislative Women (NOBEL/Women); member of the Commission on the Status of Women; Senate appointee of the Social Services Advisory Board National Commission to Prevent Mortality; Vice Chair NCSL—Assembly on State Issues Committee. Watson is single and has no children.

TERRI WRIGHT Currently director of women's health for the state of Michigan, Wright has directed a family planning clinic; coordinated health education for Planned Parenthood; headed AIDS education for the State of Connecticut, and was director of women's health for the State of Georgia. Wright is divorced and the mother of a young son.

PART I
EARLY ROOTS

A people without knowledge of its history
is like a tree without roots.

—MARCUS GARVEY

CHAPTER 1

THE BLACK FAMILY

"My father insisted that his children learn a skill and spend time on a job, but we could choose [which] job . . . Because my father was in the auto repair business, those were the skills I was [first] taught. My brothers and I used [our mechanics'] skills and knowledge to earn money, frequently earning a dollar or so to jump-start cars and charge batteries for our neighbors . . . " —JENNIFER LAWSON

JENNIFER LAWSON exudes both energy and competence. Executive vice president for national programming and promotions at Public Broadcasting Services, she was responsible for selecting, distributing, and promoting a full schedule of television programs—from *Sesame Street* to the *MacNeil-Lehrer News Hour*—for the 340 member stations across the country. Like every other woman profiled in this book, Jennifer Lawson is an African American.

Lawson is the granddaughter, on her father's side, of slaves. Both parents were born in the South, her father in Bullock County, an agricultural region of Alabama, and her mother in Louisville, Kentucky. Her parents met and married in Birmingham, Alabama, where Jennifer was born. Lawson's mother attended Alabama State University, after which she taught school. As a young man, Lawson's father worked as a coal miner, and then as a steelworker in the Birmingham mills. He was later the proprietor of an auto repair business and a respected member of the community.

Jennifer Lawson credits her parents for setting her on the path that led her from Birmingham to Tuskegee Institute, where she was awarded a full academic scholarship, to her active involvement in the civil rights movement, her work as a field representative for the National Council of Negro Women, to Tanzania in East Africa, where she lived for two years, to Columbia University, where she earned her master's degree in fine arts, and finally to the corporate offices of PBS. "I had a close relationship with my parents, and each in his or her own way was a positive influence in my life. My mother was a real caring and compassionate person," Lawson recalled. "My obligation to care for and be aware of the feelings and pain of others came from my mother. [She also passed on to me] her love for books and the acquisition of knowledge.

"My father, on the other hand, encouraged me to do whatever interested me. He was a very creative person, an inventor. His only requirement was that I tackle my goals seriously. If I wanted to be a ballet dancer, I had to be willing to study and rehearse long hours. He helped me to understand the amount of work and hardship that is necessary for success. He taught me mechanical skills along with my brothers, including how to rewire electrical motors and generators." Because of her father's encouragement, Lawson developed self-confidence—and the unspoken awareness that gender, for her, would be no barrier to success.

Lawson watched her parents lead productive and useful lives, lives that made a difference not only within her family but in the larger human community. "[M]y father . . . applied for a patent for an automobile engine that would burn low-grade fuel . . . [I've always wanted] to work on projects that are bigger than I am, and to make a contribution to society, helping to create a world that is better for my own children and for others. I came into film and television because of the challenges they have to offer. I love painting. I love to solve the problems that artists face. I also enjoy writing. The written word and art come together in film and television."

FAMILY VALUES

In any child's life, parents and extended family are the best source of stability, emotional security, love, encouragement, and fulfillment. There is no doubt that family background, as well as parental attitudes and example, all contribute to a child's level of achievement as an adult. This is not to say that children from disadvantaged family backgrounds have no chance of achievement—but their road will be much harder than that of children from caring, loving, and responsible families. "There are many values that remain deep within me because of my father's influence," pathologist and National Institutes of Health Assistant Director Dr. Vivian Pinn confided to me. "'If you have work to do, do it before you play,' my father would repeat over and over again. I don't think I resented his character building, except probably when I might have wanted to go to a party and was not allowed to go. During those times it seemed important, but when I look back I realize that his counsel was more important."

Developmental resources consultant and former radio executive Aleta Carpenter credits her mother as her source of inspiration. "My mother was comfortable with all classes of people. Her dream of returning to school and becoming a nurse was accomplished in her late thirties, but was cut short by her early death. If she had lived, my mother could have accomplished her dream of contributing more to her own community . . . I am motivated by an obligation to finish what she started. Any success that I have achieved is a tribute to her. I feel the best revenge in life is to do well, especially when it is not expected of you."

The majority of the women profiled in this book came from the sort of families that give a child the very best chances for success in life. Most of the fathers had middle-class jobs. Most owned their homes and were respected members of the community. Architect Norma Sklarek and Dr. Jewel Plummer-Cobb were daughters of physicians; Dr. Vivian Pinn's father was a schoolteacher and coach; seven others were the daughters of ministers; six were the children of successful entrepreneurs.

Some of the women who grew up during the Depression spoke about the toll it took on their lives and how their families survived by conserving their resources and adjusting their lifestyles. Norma Sklarek, America's first black woman to become a licensed architect, recalled how she and her parents had to do without during the Depression. Both parents were from the Caribbean. Her father, Dr. Walter Ernest Merrick, was born in St. Vincent, and her mother, Amy Willoughby, was born in Barbados. In 1935, Sklarek's father graduated from Howard University School of Medicine in Washington, D.C. "My father was a doctor, but we were poor in terms of money, so we did lots of things around the house ourselves. It was during the Depression, so we could not afford to hire someone else to do the work. I believe that these early childhood experiences helped develop my sense of self-sufficiency."

University president emeritus Jewel Plummer Cobb talked about a similar childhood in Chicago. "My father finished medical school the year before I was born. My mother had been, for a while, a school teacher. A child of the 1930s, I can distinctly remember my mother receiving her teacher's pay in the form of vouchers. Although I grew up in an intellectual, supportive environment with lots of love and books, this was during the Depression, and resources were limited. You would think that since my mother was a teacher and my father was a doctor, we were well-off financially, but that was not the case. My parents struggled like everyone else in the community. Even though we had food and a roof over our heads, there were sacrifices we had to make. We moved to smaller quarters because money was scarce. As a doctor, my father depended on his patients in the community to pay for his services. But, being poor black folks, his patients could not pay. Many times they paid in the form of barter; we received clothing and other items in exchange for medical services. At Christmas time the families gave us food and wonderful homemade gifts. It was just the three of us, since I had no brothers or sisters. Our relatives lived in the East, so we had just ourselves.

"One time, we were unable to continue to make payments on a piano that we were buying. That was a loss, because music was important to my mother, and I could not continue to take piano lessons. I remember when they came to take the piano away, it was a sad day in our lives. We, of course, bought another piano when things got better."

Cobb recalled that, during the '30s and '40s, if the man of the house worked regularly, a black family was considered middle class. Money, however, was only a small part of that equation. Morality, ethics, honesty, and standing in the community carried just as much if not more weight. "My mother was a proponent of quality education and was my first role model. I learned a great deal about civic activities and about the zest for living, from my mother. She made valuable contributions of her time and money in support of our community."

BREADWINNING FATHERS

Being the breadwinners for their families, black fathers looked for work wherever jobs were available. Zelma Stennis, owner of a highly successful chain of restaurants, talked about her father's efforts to support their family. "My father learned to be a tailor and worked briefly in that trade and as a nickel plater, until the Lord called him to the ministry." Reverend Leroy Moses Miles graduated from Hungersford College, a small, little-known college in Georgia founded by Booker T. Washington in his early pioneering days. Fannie Robinson, Stennis' mother, left her parents' home when she was a teenager to live with a black doctor and his family in a small town in Georgia. Fannie Robinson worked in the doctor's office and accompanied him on housecalls. She also helped deliver babies. "My mother . . . did not get the love she needed from her new family," Stennis recalled. "Her father had died, leaving her mother alone; and when she left to live with the doctor and his family, she never felt like a part of the family. Although they treated her well, and it was her decision to live with them, she always felt like an outsider. Once she got her own family, she was very loving and close to us. Not only did she care for us, but the entire neighborhood benefited from her love and kindness and knowledge of nursing—especially the pregnant women, who depended on her assistance during the birthing of their children."

Stennis told me how her parents met and married. "Someone told my father about a nice girl who worked for a doctor in a nearby town. He wrote to my mother, and they began a correspondence. Judging from the letters he wrote to her, my mother believed that my father was a good man. The two did not meet until he traveled to her home to ask for her hand in marriage." Stennis' parents migrated to Detroit, where there were better job opportunities than in the South. Because of the scarcity of jobs for black males, Reverend Miles took a custodial job with the Eureka Vacuum Cleaner Company. "They hired him to do menial work at the plant, but one day one of the white nickel platers—there were no black nickel platers—had a heart attack. Soon after, the supervisor offered the job on a temporary basis to my father, if he could learn the work. The supervisor told my father that he was being rewarded for his hard work, dependability, and loyalty. He quickly learned the job and became the first black nickel plater at the plant. He remained on the job until he left to start his own church.

"When my father decided to leave Eureka to pastor his own church, the family, at first, suffered financially. The Depression was not an easy time for the family of a minister. We had to live on a strict budget, especially since there were eventually eight of us children. My father dedicated his life to his church and his family. He was a morally strong, hardworking man. He took no foolishness from us kids. My mother was a housewife; her principal occupation was birthing and raising children. With so many of us in the family, we were raised to be responsible, independent individuals."

Aleta Carpenter's father, who had only a ninth-grade education, worked at a variety of skilled and semiskilled jobs. At one time, he laid carpet during the day and drove a taxicab at night. Aleta's mother did not begin her nursing career until she was in her mid-thirties. Carpenter, who has managed to enjoy success across several quite different careers, evidently picked up a lot of her flexibility and optimism from the women in her family: Her great-grandmother, who lived to be a hundred and three, returned to school to learn to read and write at the age of ninety-nine. "My parents' differences caused many arguments in our home, and eventually led to their separation and divorce after twenty-three years together. The underlying cause was money, which is the root of dissension in many families. My father did not want my mother to return to school or to work. He believed it was the husband's responsibility to take care of his family."

Terri Wright is the director of women's health for the state of Michigan. Her father left St. Elizabeth in Jamaica as a teenager, spending the latter part of his youth with relatives in England, where he attended a culinary academy. When he came to the United States in his twenties, he found work as a cook and later as a chef in New York City restaurants. Wright's mother came to New York directly from Jamaica. "Many young men in Jamaica traveled to England to seek higher education and jobs. Jamaica was an English colony, and it was natural that many Jamaicans went to England. My parents, who were introduced by friends from Jamaica, came to the United States because of the dream America holds for immigrants. They pursued the American dream."

Wright's parents married soon after meeting. At the beginning of their marriage, they lived with relatives, while saving enough money to "get on their feet." Wright's mother worked as a seamstress, later opening her own dressmaking and alterations shop. "After several difficult years in her dress shop, my mother worked in nursing before I persuaded her to follow me to Atlanta." Wright was a teenager growing up in Queens when her parents separated and divorced. "My father did not divorce himself from us kids. He recognized my mother's role as the mother of his children and treated her with respect and admiration. He took good care of us all."

D. Antoinette Handy, retired director of music for the National Endowment for the Arts, told me that her father often reminded his children of the hard times he endured growing up in the South. "Although he grew up poor, my father saw education as the key to a better life. His goal was to become a Methodist minister, which he finally achieved through determination, sacrifice, and perseverance. He was proud of the fact that while he was a student at Tuskegee Institute he had the opportunity to sing at the funeral of Booker T. Washington, the founding president of the century-old institute, which was established in 1881.

"While my father pastored the Scott Methodist Church in Pasadena, California, one day he received a surprise visit from Albert Einstein. This was a real occasion, since Einstein seldom visited churches. A few days later, an international newspaper came out with a photograph of my father with Einstein and his wife, and other community leaders." Handy also recalled her father's feelings about the honorary doctor of divinity degrees he received. "He never felt comfortable using the title of doctor of divinity. He felt the greatest title was that of 'Reverend.' In fact, he called his D.D., 'donated dignity.'"

Handy spoke with pride of her father, the Rev. William Talbot Handy, and her mother, Darthney Pauline Pleasant Handy, whom she described as a brilliant and talented woman. "My mother postponed her own college education until my father achieved his educational goals. We watched with great pride the day she received her degree. All of the family members were deeply touched as she marched across that stage to receive her bachelor of arts degree. I was nine years old. She did not let her college studies interfere with her duties as a wife and mother. She was able to balance all three reasonably well."

Handy credits her professional success to her parents' counsel, their respect for education, and the solid moral foundation that was built in their family. Her mother died in 1980 at the age of 92, her father in 1983, at the age of 87. "They lived a full, rich life, were married sixty-three years, and lived to see the results of their sacrifices to educate their children." Handy's brother is a retired Bishop in the United Methodist Church, with jurisdiction over the Missouri area. "My brother received three college degrees—a bachelor of arts, a bachelor of divinity, and a master of sacred theology—as well as several honorary doctorates." Handy's sister completed her bachelor of arts, a master of music degree in piano, and a Ph.D. She is retired from a professorship at the University of Minnesota. A fourth sibling died when he was thirteen; Handy believes that he was the most brilliant of all the children.

The family of award-winning children's book writer Eloise Greenfield was part of the exodus of blacks who made their way from the deep South to cities north of the Mason-Dixon Line during the 1930s. Soon after Greenfield was born in Palmele, North Carolina, her family migrated to Washington, D.C. Her father first came alone to look for work and a place for his family to live, finding a job as a porter for the People's Drug Store, an old and established landmark in the capital city. Three months later, he sent for his wife and children.

"After working for a time at People's Drug Store, my father was able to qualify for a much-sought-after job with the Interior Department. The federal government offered security and better wages. My mother, Lessie Jones Little, worked briefly during World War II, but they both agreed that being home with the children was more important than the money she made. She was able, however, to supplement my father's salary by sewing for families in the neighborhood. When we were older, my mother returned to work, first as a clerk typist, and later as a coder for the Department of the Army. Having had childhood dreams to become a published writer, she finally fulfilled those dreams after retiring from the federal government."

Greenfield's mother became a writer in her sixties, after Greenfield herself had become a published writer. "Finally my mother's dreams to have some of her works published were fulfilled. We did two books together, and her book of poetry, *Children of Long Ago,* was published posthumously—but she knew it was going to be published."

Greenfield's grandmother, who lived in Norfolk, Virginia, also wrote short stories. "I sent her magazines that my stories appeared in, and she began to write little autobiographical essays about her own life. When she moved to Washington, D.C. in 1970 to live with my parents, she brought her stories with her. She was really very shy about sharing them, but I was excited about her efforts, and encouraged her, suggesting topics for her to cover." After her grandmother died, Greenfield set to work with her mother on organizing and adding to her grandmother's writing. "That is how *ChildTimes* came about. It is the story of each of our childhoods, a three-generation memoir."

HOMEMAKING MOTHERS AND OTHERS

Primarily because of the times in which they grew up, most of the women I interviewed had mothers who were housewives. If their mothers worked, it was because they were either divorced or widowed, or had a temporary special purpose that created the need for extra income, such as assisting with the cost of college for their spouse or children or helping to buy a home. Restaurateur Zelma Stennis recalls, "My mother was too busy [with] us eight kids to find time to work outside the home." Dr. Cynthia Shepard Perry, former U.S. Ambassador to Sierra Leone and Burundi, put it succinctly: "My mother, of course, had the hardest job of all—raising a family."

For the single mothers, staying home was not an option. My own childhood was filled with personal adjustments after my parents divorced, before my mother's remarriage. She was able to use her skills as a seamstress to work for the federal government, making clothing for poor children. Because she had to leave home at six o'clock each weekday morning, I suddenly found myself at the age of seven with a lot of responsibilities. I had to get breakfast for my younger brother and myself, make sure we were washed and properly dressed, get us to school on time, and stay home from school every other Wednesday to make sure that my mother's civil service check wasn't stolen from the mailbox. After the mailman arrived, I took the bus downtown to meet my mother when she left work at two. The first thing we did was to go to Weingarten's, a large grocery chain, to stock up on food until the next paycheck arrived.

Art scholar Dr. Mary Jane Hewitt tells of her mother's struggle to raise four children after her husband's death. "She was so cared for by my father that she knew nothing about making a living. She didn't even know what a mortgage was. My father had built the house we lived in, but we lost it soon after he died. At first she didn't know how to manage money, but she quickly learned the hard way."

Hewitt was born in Kansas City, Kansas, just a few months after her father died. His thirty-year-old widow raised their son and three daughters alone, never remarrying. The daughter of a rebel who established residency in Canada to escape the racism in the United States, Hewitt's mother was intolerant of all race-based limits to personal freedom, and she taught her children to embrace the same principles.

"Because of my mother's schooling and growing up in Canada, she was a master seamstress and an excellent cook. When my father died she had to depend on her domestic training in order to feed her family. She cooked, made draperies, sewed, and did all kinds of domestic work for wealthy white families, including upholstering their furniture. My mother became so capable that she was intimidating. For example, she would hire an electrician to do some work, watch him carefully, and, from then on, did the work herself. She did the same thing with the plumber and the carpenter. She could do anything and make anything."

Hewitt's mother later worked as a restroom matron for Northwest Airlines. "Although the job was menial, it gave her a chance to earn a steady income and to be able to contribute toward Social Security. Northwest had a retirement plan, so by the time she retired, she was very comfortably situated. We were all grown by then, so all of her money was hers, and she proceeded to invest in real estate, buying old homes in the community, fixing them up, and then reselling them at a profit. A few years after she retired, my mother was diagnosed with Alzheimer's disease, which kept her from fully developing her new talent in real estate."

The late Ruth Washington, president and publisher of the Los Angeles *Sentinel*, also had a mother who raised her family alone. Washington was only four years old when her father was killed in combat in World War I. "My mother was confronted with the harsh reality of supporting a family of three young girls without a husband. She took stock of what she could do to make a living and decided to become a cook, a skill she had learned from her mother. She worked hard in the kitchens of wealthy white families to support us children. She went to school to learn catering and was able to plan meals for 3,000 people as easily as for ten. As we got older, all of the family worked. Our family was close, and we were fortunate to have aunts and uncles and cousins in our neighborhood to call on when needed."

I found it interesting that many of the mothers were able to use homemaking skills taught them in their youth, either at home or at school, to see them through such emergencies as divorce or the death of a spouse. Artist Betye Saar's mother was another case in point. Saar's parents were both students at UCLA in the 1930s. Her father graduated from the university, but her mother decided to quit during her senior year. Saar's father, Jefferson Brown, worked for many years as a salesman for Golden State Insurance and for a time as Sunday School Superintendent for the Independent Church of Los Angeles; he also worked at the 28th Street YMCA. Both parents were active in the Urban League and the NAACP. "My father was working on his master's degree when he passed away," Saar said. "After my father died, my mother was left with three children to raise and educate. She worked as a seamstress to support us . . . [until] she remarried and had two children from her second marriage."

BUILDING A FOUNDATION

Most psychologists agree that basic personality structures are developed as early as five or six years of age. All children need stimulating environments, with family and community support systems that are trustworthy, caring, and encouraging. When this type of socialization is established at a young age, strong foundations are built that allow children to flower to their fullest potential.

These theories are certainly borne out by the lives of the women profiled here. About a third of them mentioned both parents as strong, positive influences. Fathers were cited as role models by some of the women, while the rest felt that their mothers and extended family members—grandparents, aunts, cousins—or role models from within the community—neighbors or teachers—were tremendous sources of encouragement and inspiration.

The father of Beverly Hills pediatrician Brenda Bass was an army officer, which meant that he was often absent from the day-to-day lives of his two daughters. It was only during Bass' years at college and medical school that she and her father developed a closer relationship. "During my youth, my father's military duties kept him from being with us as much as the family would have liked. It was my mother who took care of our daily needs. My father's influence was more visible after high school. He helped me crystallize things that were important to me as an adult. We discussed such things as career and life goals, and the steps that must be taken to meet my goals. He gave me that kind of guidance, and I appreciated his interest."

Significantly, the majority of the women grew up in intact families. Even among those parents who were divorced, many did not separate until their children were older.

The parents of investment banker Iris Rideau were a notable exception. They divorced when Rideau, an only child, was still a toddler. Rideau continued to have a loving relationship with her father but never felt secure after he left. Married at fifteen, Rideau raised a child with the help of her mother, worked in a factory, and went to night school for her high school equivalency certificate until she got her life on track—eventually becoming president of her own highly successful insurance and investment banking firm. Her father's absences for long periods of time, and then his sudden reappearances, created scars that have never completely healed. Each time she and her mother welcomed him with open arms, they knew that he would leave again to chase his personal dreams. "Since my father did not live with us, there was always that anxiety that I might not see him again. He took care of us to a certain extent, but it was apparent that he didn't realize the pain that he was causing by his absences. I had this tremendous fantasy about my father returning to live with us permanently, but that never happened. It was really my mother and my extended family who were there for me."

Ambassador Cynthia Perry says that she was close to both her parents. "I received my creative talent from my father and my pragmatism from my mother. During my youth, both parents played important roles that are important to me as a adult. Neither of them had a formal education, but were aware of the advantage of an education. Most of the black families in the community had little education but held it in high regard."

Perry was born in Terre Haute, Indiana, where her father, George William Norton, worked as a bus driver for the Vigo County school system. Her mother was a homemaker. "Although my father had a good-paying job, there were ten children in the family to feed, clothe, and shelter. He was also a musician and an artist who painted in oils. Those were his preoccupations. In addition, he was a hunter and a lover of the outdoors. The days of the Depression were times for adjusting our lives economically and for helping others. Our lives were enriched by the sacrifices we made.

"I was a middle child, coming along after a sister and four brothers. My brothers and sisters felt that my parents favored me and thought that I was given special privileges that were not given them. I disagree. I think the difference was that I took advantage of opportunities that were offered me."

Perry's story points to the significance other adults can play in young girls' lives. She cites both a black elementary school teacher and her high school principal as great influences on her career path. The elementary school teacher nurtured not only racial pride in each of her students but a strong concept of individual identity as well. "My teacher awakened in us the will to achieve as individuals despite the odds. On the other hand, my high school principal is the reason why I chose to become an ambassador. It was because of his knowledge, encouragement, and guidance that I eventually reached my goal."

When Perry decided to return to college, after marriage and four children, it was her high school principal whom she contacted. During one of their career discussions, he asked what she would like to be twenty years down the road. She answered, "An ambassador." Instead of laughing at her, the principal encouraged Perry to follow her dream, even though the journey was one that no woman from her situation—either white or black—had ever undertaken before.

In addition to a supportive family, State Senator Diane Watson also had the good fortune to encounter a teacher who cared. "Birdilee Bright saw potential in each of her students and helped us reach it. She never accepted anything less than what she thought each student could accomplish. For her I would wash my shoelaces and shine my shoes everyday. She challenged us. Teachers like Birdilee Bright helped in the formation of my own philosophy and my choice of a career. While I was a member of the Los Angeles School Board, I named a hall after her—I couldn't name a school in her honor because she was still living."

President of her own consulting firm, as well as president of the Association of Black Women Entrepreneurs, Dolores Ratcliffe tells a similar tale. "When I was growing up, there were teachers like Dorothy Vena Johnson who had the qualities I admired. She was an outstanding human being and only one of two black teachers at my elementary school. I decided in the third grade that I would be like her; she was a published poet and encouraged us students to write poetry and to be the best we could be. I had the pleasure, many years later, to tell her that I became a teacher because of her." Later in her career, Ratcliffe led a successful campaign to have a high school named after Dorothy Vena Johnson.

Religion played an important role in the young lives of many of the women who tell their stories here. Reverend Ella Mitchell, an Atlanta Baptist minister and the daughter of a Presbyterian minister, was allowed the freedom of choosing whatever road her dreams led her to follow. "My father encouraged our development. Each of us girls had one day with him; there were three daughters and a cousin who lived with us. We could talk about anything. I remember the exciting times he and I had when I was in high school. We regularly read plays by William Shakespeare. My father was a wonderful father and a talented minister. I knew at an early age that I would be a minister like him, and I led my life with that in mind."

Reverend Leontine Kelly was the first African American woman ever to be elected a Bishop in the United Methodist Church. "I was fortunate to have parents as positive role models. Later it was my brother, a minister, who helped me. I admired his preaching style, and patterned my own preaching style after his."

General manager of the Los Angeles Department of Recreation and Parks, Jackie Tatum gives credit to both her mother and grandmother for the early guidance that helped build her strong commitment to service and accomplishment. Both mother and grandmother were college graduates who became teachers. "There was that constant pursuit of excellence, a legacy they passed on to me. They also believed that travel was educating. When I had the opportunity to travel during my youth, I became aware of the advantages and disadvantages of black people in different parts of the country. My grandmother believed in exposing me to an array of experiences, which helped me to understand that life can be difficult as well as enjoyable. She explained to me that there were problems that we must face in one way or another. Only those with the strength to face and overcome challenges will survive."

INSPIRING FATHERS

Several of the women I interviewed mentioned closer relationships with their father than with their mother, and it is an intriguing notion to ponder: Do girls have a greater chance of succeeding in the workplace if they identify more with their father who worked outside the home than with a stay-at-home mother? Concert singer Henrietta Davis Blackmon told me, "My father held a cherished place in my life. He encouraged me continually . . . He gave me the safety, the security, and the consistency to fly as high as my wings would take me."

Restauranteur Zelma Stennis grew up in a strict religious environment. Her father was old-fashioned, morally strong, and hardworking, and yet showed tenderness and sensitivity in the way he encouraged her musical talent. She recalls him slipping bus fare and money for piano lessons under her pillow as she slept. Her mother, more practically minded, thought that Stennis' dream of becoming a concert pianist was "a waste of time and money."

World-renowned architect Norma Sklarek was the only child of a physician. "Although both my parents adored me, I did lots of things with my father that ordinarily girls did not do—like going fishing, painting the house, and doing carpentry work . . . Perhaps because of my father's influence, the typical female careers did not appeal to me. My grades were such that I could consider any profession, but I had an interest in art, the sciences, and math. One day my father said to me, 'What about architecture?' I knew absolutely nothing about architecture, but it seemed to embody each of my interests, and I considered his suggestion."

Jewel Plummer Cobb, President Emeritus of California State University at Fullerton, received her Ph.D. in cell physiology. She was also the only child of a physician father. "My father always encouraged me in whatever I wanted to do. When I was young, my relationship with him was much better than with my mother. My mother and I tended to be in competition with each other. Of course, as I got older, she and I had many things in common, including our educational interests . . . While I was in college, my mother returned to college, and we received our degrees at the same time."

Iris Rideau spoke candidly about how her parents' divorce affected her relationship with them. "Whenever my father returned to my home in New Orleans to see us, there was that competition between my mother and me for his attention. She did not like having to rear me alone and wanted him with her. When it was time for him to return to Chicago, where he lived, both she and I wanted to go with him. But that never happened, so there was this frustration that affected our daughter-mother relationship. When I got older, there was a healing. My mother and I are now very close."

For all of the women profiled here, family played a major role in their ability to function autonomously and served as a secure base from which they were able to thrive both intellectually and emotionally. The family unit—whether or not this included an intact mother-and-father pair—empowered these women to be successful in their careers as well as their personal lives. With their love and nurturing, example, and encouragement, parents help develop a child's inner sense of being inherently good and inherently valuable. With such foundations to build on, no mountain is indeed ever too high.

CHAPTER 2

BLACK DISCIPLINE

"My father ... often told us that his guidance was for our own good ... to help us cope with the problems of society ... You had to attend church and, while there, do nothing that would reflect negatively on the family. Also at breakfast, lunch, and dinner, we were required to be there. We sat around the table and discussed the Bible. My father was 'ultra' in moral behavior and ethical standards ... I continue to live by those standards today." —ZELMA STENNIS

ZELMA STENNIS, president and CEO of Golden Birds Incorporated in Los Angeles, is one of the few African American women to head an important family-owned restaurant chain. She and her husband, Bill, opened their first restaurant in March 1953 in their hometown of Detroit, Michigan. In March 1958, they relocated to Los Angeles. Stennis handles the finances, develops the annual budget, oversees the office operations, and makes sure that produce and equipment are of the highest quality. Before his death in 1993, her husband, Bill, handled locations and maintenance and the construction of new restaurants. They brought their oldest son, Michael, into the business as vice president and chief operating officer.

For our interview, I met Stennis at her home in Hancock Park, an affluent community near the Wilshire district of Los Angeles. The

Stennis' home was previously owned by Nat King Cole, who graced the formerly all-white neighborhood with its first black family. When the Coles moved into the community, the Hancock Park homeowners protested loud and long. No matter that Nat King Cole was a successful recording artist who had his own popular television show, he and his family were attacked by their neighbors with racist epithets and hate mail. By the time the Stennis family bought their home, Hancock Park had become more ethnically mixed and more receptive to minorities.

Stennis, the mother of four sons, has never forgotten the strict religious environment in which she was nurtured. Her minister father divided his life between his church and his family. His eight children were raised to be both responsible and independent—and they were not even allowed to play with other children who did not meet his rigorous standards. One day he found out that Zelma's best friend did not have a father at home, and made her end the friendship.

"Each child in my family had chores to perform and individual responsibilities. There was work to be done on Saturday mornings, followed by fun in the afternoon when the chores were completed. The house was cleaned, and so was the church where my father preached. Then, the Model A Ford (later replaced by a Chrysler) had to be cleaned and polished. We would clean the wheels and polish the outside of the car until we could see our faces in it. When we finished our chores, our father rewarded us by taking us riding in the gleaming Model A Ford. Most of the time we went to the park to play and picnic. On the way to the park, we stopped at the market to buy bologna, rye bread, and sodas.

"My father taught us at an early age that you never get credit for what you know or what you do; but if it's good and beneficial, do it anyway."

TO BE SEEN AND NOT HEARD

African American parents have a long-standing reputation for being stern disciplinarians. In a recent study of 204 black mothers, forty-two percent had spanked their young children in the week before the study. The report found that inner-city mothers were more likely to spank than well-to-do suburban mothers. Had these researchers delved more deeply, they would have found an interesting historical rationale for black discipline in America.

From slavery to the present, the old Biblical aphorism, "Spare the rod and spoil the child," has been taken to heart by many black families. The tradition of harsh discipline reaches all the way back to the history of slavery, when parents exerted strong control over their children to protect them from much more dire consequences at the hands of plantation masters or overseers. If a young slave resisted authority or asserted himself in any way, he was likely to be cruelly beaten or even killed.

After the Emancipation Proclamation, black American parents still had to protect their children, especially in the South, from the life-and-death dangers sanctioned by Jim Crow laws created to keep black people in their place. It was preferable to teach your child the rigors of accepted social behavior through strict and sometimes harsh discipline than to see your child beaten or brutally lynched by an angry white mob.

By today's standards, parents of my generation and those before me would be considered child abusers. When I was growing up, you didn't talk back, and you didn't sass your elders. Children were supposed to be seen and not heard, at least in the company of adults. "Do it and suffer the consequences" was a phrase I often heard in my community. Some child development authorities call this "Traditional Black Discipline." Traditional or not, you just didn't stand back with your hands on your hips and tell your parents where to go. You'd be "asking for it," and "it" meant one of two things, depending on your family: a verbal tongue-lashing or a corporal assault. Today's far more gentle practice of "time out" was not part of the disciplinary agenda I grew up with.

Research conducted in 1979 by Diana Baurind identified the three most prevalent discipline patterns in American families: *authoritarian, authoritative, and permissive.*

- *Authoritarian parents* set standards of control and behavior in accordance with the way they think their child should behave, without necessarily providing explanations. If the rules are broken, the child expects to be punished. Punishments are immediate and non-negotiable and may include beatings.

• *Authoritative parents* tend to maintain more of a give-and-take relationship with their children, in that they will listen to the child's point of view. Rules are explained beforehand, are enforced with consistency, and there are set punishments when rules are broken.

• *Permissive parents* are noncontrolling and nondemanding. There are few expectations for the child to live up to in terms of helping with household responsibilities or following particular standards of behavior in public or private.

Although many black parents even today believe that the authoritarian mode of discipline is most effective in terms of teaching respect and correcting antisocial behavior, the empirical literature supports the second model as working best: parents who are supportive and nurturing, but still assert their power and control. Based on Baurind's definition of parental patterns, I found that the pattern experienced by the majority of the women I interviewed was closest to the authoritative model. "We could not talk on the phone for hours like teenagers do today," said Aleta Carpenter." We could not make or take phone calls after nine o'clock in the evening; we had to be at home after dark; we couldn't date until a certain age; you didn't talk back; and you didn't smoke in the house. Nothing. Those were my parents' rules, and we followed them."

Some of the parents who recognized leadership ability in their children allowed some freedom of choice with guidance. Ambassador Cynthia Shepard Perry's parents were not permissive, but at the same time they did not try to control her life—which would have, she believes, caused her to rebel. "I think they used different methods of parenting for each of us children, according to our needs. I was considered a bright child, and was treated as such.

"I graduated from high school when I was seventeen and entered Indiana University soon after. I left college in my freshman year, which disappointed my parents. You see, I fell in love and was married before my eighteenth birthday. After I left college, I started having babies, three in a row. It was not until after I had my fourth child that I again entered college to finish my bachelor's degree."

Children's book author and poet Eloise Greenfield recalls that she was allowed to speak freely and express personal opinions as a child—within the framework of certain restrictions and rules. "We could not be rude. We had strict curfews, and there were limits to where we could go and could not go with friends. Morals and ethics were important to my parents. Church and Sunday School were also an important part of our lives. We went regularly to both. I did not call on religion directly when I was learning to write, but spirituality is very important. We can use it to guide us toward what is ethical—in other words, [to help us decide] what is right and what is wrong."

Jennifer Lawson of PBS told me that her parents used a mixed style in rearing their children. "They were neither too permissive nor too authoritarian. While my father insisted that we children attend church every Sunday, he did not dictate what we believed nor the church we attended. Instead he encouraged a curiosity about church and religion. My father absolutely insisted that we go to some kind of church, but we were left to make our own choices. As a consequence, I went to the Unitarian church, the Methodist church, the Baptist Church, and the Catholic church. At different times I was baptized as a Baptist and as a Catholic, and I was married by an Episcopal bishop in a Quaker meeting house."

Jackie Tatum, who runs the vast Los Angeles Parks and Recreation system, experienced a somewhat more permissive upbringing than many of the other women profiled here. Reared by her mother and grandmother, Tatum describes their particular nonverbal form of guidance. "I was receptive to any suggestions they made in directing my activities. They had a way of looking at me, and I knew what it meant. No spanking or anything like that—just looks. It still works."

It was evident during my interviews that the women felt a clear delineation between parent and children during their childhoods. Many of the fathers were seen as authoritarian heads of families who emphasized respectability at home and in the community and the building of character. Singer Henrietta Davis-Blackmon, the third daughter of a Baptist minister, felt that her life was structured but not completely controlled by her father. "My father was a little more strict with my older sisters than with me. By the time I arrived, he must have gotten tired of being the authoritarian figure."

Atlanta Baptist minister Reverend Ella Mitchell, a Presbyterian minister's daughter, believes that she restricted her own behavior more than her parents did. "My sisters often told me, 'You do everything Mama tells you to do.' I followed my parents' rules plus those I made myself. While my sister might have sipped a little wine at someone's home when we got older, I would not. I was also careful about the way I dressed. My sisters called me a fuddy-duddy, because I did not use lipstick or rouge or nail polish. They wondered if I would ever grow up to be an attractive young lady.

"When we were growing up, my mother was more strict than my father. Mama was very, very strict. We did not play cards in our family— no, no, no. There was no alcohol of any kind in our home. There was no smoking in our home. We were not allowed to go to the movies, because movies were segregated. My parents did not want us girls to sit in the balcony, where they segregated black people from white people."

Actor Donzaleigh Abernathy, daughter of the Reverend Ralph David Abernathy, recalled that her father was never the disciplinarian. "When I did something wrong, he would tell me how much it had broken his heart. This made me feel terribly guilty. He was so loving and so kind and affectionate and communicative. My mother was both disciplinarian and nurturer. She is a woman's woman, who helped me become a lady. She nurtured the femininity and the strength in me. Above all, she taught me independence. 'Never walk in front nor behind, but beside your man.'

"During my childhood, in addition to her nurturing, she was also the disciplinarian, and she was very strict. I guess my mother was the reason my sister and I had the reputation for being 'good girls.' She felt that it was important to be a lady. She instilled in us that we had to be refined, dignified young women. She was emphatic about our learning and being able to read. During the summer vacation, we would study from the

World Book Encyclopedia. In the back of the dictionary were levels of words that they suggested a child learn from kindergarten through grade twelve. Every summer we had to sit still and learn those words, their meaning, and their usage. My mother was there every day, a kind of hands-on person.

"Mother also nurtured the arts in us: We took ballet. I was so much in love with ballet that I thought that I would become a ballerina. My mother said, 'Oh no, you won't. You are going to learn other things.' So we started piano lessons, which I rebelled against. I was a defiant, strong-willed little girl, which my daddy admired.

"My mother was a teacher until [the birth of] her first child, Ralph David, Jr., who died in his crib. His death was a tremendous strain on Mother. She stopped teaching with her next pregnancy and became a full-time mother, but she continued to work in the [civil rights] Movement. She taught people how to read and write so they could register to vote. We didn't have the right to vote in the South back then. Many African Americans in the South, because of inferior education, were illiterate. Just as we have illiteracy today, we had it then, but on a much larger scale. But no matter how hard she worked in the Movement, my mother was always there for us—she did not forget her parenting responsibilities."

State Senator Diane Watson remembers her father as being extremely strict. "He came from a devoutly religious family, his mother having been reared in a Catholic convent for thirteen years. When he told us that it was time to go to bed, there was no question about it. When he asked us to stop talking, we stopped talking. When he told us that there were no activities except church, we went to church. When he said we should eat all our food, we ate all our food. We never questioned him. We were disciplined early and often.

"My mother was just the opposite. She was fun-loving and warm and exposed us children to many varied experiences, including extensive travel. Once, she took me, and my father took my sister Barbara, and we met up in Kansas City. I can still remember that experience. After they were divorced, my mother continued to expose us to many activities that helped to shape our character. We took train trips and stayed in hotels. During the summer, we girls were sent to stay in Fresno, where we picked grapes for spending change. On the Fourth of July, the family went to Val Verde picnic grounds north of Los Angeles or to Riverside to visit relatives. My mother believed that exposure to different environments and different people was important to the development of young children."

Vivian Pinn, past president of the National Medical Association, grew up in Lynchburg, Virginia, the only child of two high school teachers, both of them born in Virginia. Pinn remembers her parents as hardworking and loving. "Although my father was a teacher, he worked twelve months a year—during the summer he worked in sports and recreation. My mother also worked all year.

"Despite the fact that both my parents worked long hours, we were a close-knit family. We had a large family on both sides, and it was a great loss to me and our family when my mother died. I was nineteen and a sophomore at Wellesley College. After my mother died, my father supported me in all my needs, emotionally and financially, until I finished medical school. It was a tremendous financial sacrifice for him. Because of my father's love, which he gave freely, and his encouragement, I felt I owed it to him and my mother to study hard and do well in all my classes at college and at medical school.

"My father was the strict disciplinarian, not only toward me, but toward everyone around him. Although he was firm, I did not find it restrictive, because everybody knew how he was. All my friends knew him, because he taught at our high school. In fact they sort of respected him for it. I did not rebel too much, because I also respected him. Although he was strict, he was fair, and he was not abusive. He had very firm ideas about success and how one develops confidence and self-esteem. Even now, since his death, I sometimes catch myself thinking, 'Gee whiz, I'd better get home—it's getting late.'"

Philanthropist Eileen Norton had four adults directing her life and looking after her needs. Her father and mother divorced when Norton was a child. "My father's family migrated from Texas and lived in Colorado for a while. His family is now in Bakersfield. I grew up with my mother, her two brothers, and my grandfather. I was an only child among all those adults.

"Sometimes I felt smothered by all those adults watching over me. I know now that their sheltering me was their way of helping me to develop in a direction they thought best. There were a few kids in the neighborhood that I was allowed to play with, but when I was at home I played by myself. My mother gave me everything she thought I needed, like clothes and toys and books—things like that. I had all this attention, but I wanted less attention and more time to be a kid and be with other kids."

Vivian Bowser, past president of the Texas State Teacher's Association, recalled that her parents maintained a wonderful balance in their style of parenting. "I believe my parents complemented each other very well, in that my mother used a hard and heavy hand, and my father was more moderate." Her mother's philosophy, Bowser explains, was Biblical in its origin. "For instance, if I came to her and said, 'Mary's parents are allowing her to go to such and such,' my mother would say, 'For me and my house, you will do it this way.' Although my mother was strict, both parents gave us opportunities to excel. They believed that the development of a child's self-esteem and . . . recognition of self-worth must begin in a family environment. I agree with that. Children must be encouraged to be the best that they can be. Compliments are important. All of these attributes are important in instilling in young people that they are worthy. But it has to be sincere. Young people have a keen and uncanny sense for detecting insincerity."

Bowser's family gave her freedom with direction. Her father held the job of caretaker for Houston's Emancipation Park, a large public park in the third ward, created for blacks in the community. The Bowser home was located on the premises and was a gathering place for many of the kids in the neighborhood, who all treated Bowser's parents as second parents. Her father could be relied on to help families with problems, especially when sons of single mothers got out of hand. Both parents reached out into the community to help in every way they could. "It was a close-knit community, where everybody cared about each other and looked out for each other's kids."

DISCIPLINE IN FAMILIES ORIGINATING OUTSIDE THE UNITED STATES

Four of the women profiled here had immigrant parents. Art scholar Mary Jane Hewitt's mother grew up in Canada. "She was my mother and father, because my father died while my mother was pregnant with me. We are both Scorpios, very strong-willed people. I'm the youngest, and the most confrontational of the four children. My mother had Victorian morals and taboos. The three other children would defy her covertly. I would defy her restrictions openly, so we always had a tug-of-war going on. We, of course, loved each other, and we were friends, but there were those strong wills that were pitted against each other."

As a teenager, Terri Wright, Director of Women's Health for the State of Michigan, found it hard being reared by West Indian Jamaican parents in an American culture. "I struggled to live biculturally. Some of the things my American friends did, like dating at an early age, were unacceptable to Jamaican families. My friends dated at fourteen and fifteen. My father would not allow me to date until I was seventeen. The boys who wanted to take me out had to ask my father two weeks ahead. He wanted to know where we were going, how long we would be gone, and how we planned to get back. My dating and other social activities became more comfortable when I developed a friendship with a Jamaican girl. She had two older brothers—so when we went out with her brothers, my father gave his approval.

"Most of my social life revolved around family activities. Every Friday night my friends came to my house, as my mother loved to entertain. We also had different outside activities. I remember my father taking us to see the Jackson Five at Madison Square Garden. In winter we went ice skating on Saturdays at Prospect Park or the Rockefeller Center. We went on occasion to Radio City Music Hall; and at Christmas and Easter, lots of family activities were planned.

"My parents held strong opinions about values and justice. My father, who was fair-skinned, experienced a great deal of racism in England. Although he was not what is called afrocentric, he had strong opinions about equal rights for black people—or 'colored people,' as my parents called black people. He felt strongly about the ability to speak out about injustice and had positive feelings about Malcolm X, Martin Luther King, and John F. Kennedy. Those were people whom he admired and talked about often. I believe the greatest thing he instilled in me was a strong sense of justice and of self."

The parents of *Essence* editor-in-chief Susan Taylor also came from strict Victorian English backgrounds. Her father was born in Saint Kitts, and her mother in Trinidad. "My parents were middle-aged when I was born. My mother was thirty-seven, and my father was eleven years older than she. We children were expected to speak properly, behave in a proper manner, and treat our elders with great respect. We knew where the lines were drawn and what our responsibilities were.

"My parents owned a ladies' dress shop in the same building where we lived in Harlem. Because their business was on the premises both parents kept an eye on us. My father was right there in the store, and he could see me from every window as I played hopscotch and jumped rope with the neighborhood children."

Architect Norma Sklarek—whose parents were also West Indian—recalls that she was usually given freedom to make her own decisions. "They did not push me in any particular direction. I remember the first year at Columbia—I had a hard time because everything was so different from high school. I was working extremely hard just to stay afloat, not getting *A*s, but just trying to pass the course. I spent the summer deliberating whether or not to return to Columbia in the fall. I decided to stay, but not because of parental pressure. If I had wanted to, I could have left and studied somewhere else. My parents' only requirement was that I attend college near home. I wanted to go to Howard University in Washington, D.C., because I thought there was more social life at Howard, but my father wouldn't think of it."

WHAT WORKS BEST?

In her research on the socialization of young children, Diana Baurind found that parents designated as authoritative had the most achievement-oriented daughters. But permissive parents—those whose control was lax, who did not inhibit tomboy behavior, and who did not seek to produce sex-role conformity in girls—had daughters who were nearly as achievement-oriented and independent as those from authoritative parents. Authoritarian parents tended to have the most socially conforming, least successful daughters. Baurind cautions that her findings are most relevant for white, middle-class families and cannot necessarily be extrapolated to explain behavior patterns in other families. She concludes that if black families were viewed by white norms they would appear deviant; yet judged on their own merits, the so-called black authoritarian methods seem to produce assertive and independent young women.

The patterns most prevalent among the parents of the women profiled in this book—ranging between strict authoritarian discipline and freedom with direction—would seem to confirm Baurind's findings about discipline and success in black families. Certainly all of these women would be described by any observer as confident, assertive, and independent—no one of them would ever have achieved so much without possessing all of these qualities in abundance. And yet I think it would be misleading to recommend the strict disciplinary standards of these families as a model for raising children of the present generation. Most authorities in child development would argue that authoritarian modes of discipline involving corporal punishment or verbal abuse are not only outmoded but unnecessarily cruel. Discipline is highly important and even crucial to the future success of a child, but there are many ways to achieve discipline without practicing abuse. Readers who are interested in exploring this subject further should refer to reading list at the end of this book which incorporates some of the better works available.

No matter what the race or culture, the family environment serves as a secure base from which a child can formulate and practice positive life-skills. It was obvious in my interviews that each of these women had benefited from the encouragement, support, and love of their parents—as well as from the parentally imposed restrictions they experienced as children. A secure sense of limits and boundaries gave each of these women a framework within which she could develop and master the skills needed to compete productively and thrive—both intellectually and emotionally—as an adult.

CHAPTER 3

SELF-ESTEEM AND
THE BLACK GIRL

"I discovered a strange kind of phenomenon from my peers in college. Most felt that I was there because of some kind of quota system. It did not matter that I had graduated cum laude—many made assumptions that I could not do certain things. My color fitted the stereotype, so they believed that I could not accomplish what they could accomplish. I guess one thing that motivated me was spite—a kind of, 'I'll show them. [Let them] see what I can do.'"
—DR. PAT COWINGS

P ART OF MY PROBLEM, in the beginning of my career," NASA researcher Pat Cowings told me, "stemmed from the fact that I earned my Ph.D. at age twenty-three—people thought I was too young to know anything . . . If you live long enough, you will get over the obstacles of youth and inexperience. But I am still a short, brown woman. I still have to contend with racism."

Cowings is a principal research investigator who heads the Psychophysiological Research Laboratory at Ames Research Center, a NASA facility north of San Francisco. Psychophysiology is the study of the relationship between the mind, behavior, and bodily mechanisms. Cowings has been working on developing a treatment for the motion sickness commonly experienced by astronauts during manned space flights, using autogenic feedback training—processes that condition people to consciously control their normally unconscious bodily responses.

Cowings always wanted to be an astronaut. She was the first American woman to receive scientist-astronaut training as part of the shuttle training program. "When I was in graduate school, some of my friends called me the Space Cadet, because I was always watching the launches and talking about space programs. During that time, I was doing graduate work in psychophysiology. Since no one rushed to make me an astronaut, the next best thing was to try to contribute something worthwhile to the space program, namely that would benefit astronauts. I knew that I could do that through NASA, so I took special pains to find out what NASA needed and how I could be useful to them. I then directed my energies and attention to making myself valuable to the organization.

"Professor Hans Mark at UC Davis taught the special graduate courses I needed, and was also, coincidentally, the director at Ames. When I first came to Ames, I worked in various research assistant positions. Later I obtained a post-doctorate fellowship with the National Research Council, which allowed me to work full-time at NASA. Four years later I was hired as a research scientist and head of the Psychophysiological Research Laboratories. Mae Jemison, M.D., the first black female astronaut, and three Japanese astronauts were my subjects on Spacelab-J, which flew in September 1992.

"I quickly learned that working in the space program was not a piece of cake. I'm—how should I say this? I'm from the North, right? And my parents somewhat sheltered me. I knew about prejudice and chauvinism and stuff like that. I read about it and saw it on television. But it disturbed me a lot when I had to encounter it firsthand. I'm not talking about anybody burning a cross on my lawn or anything like that—but things like having my experiment removed from the manifest, because I was not considered a 'serious' scientist. Some individuals at another space center made concerted efforts to remove me as a principal investigator. They did not, quote, feel that I was the right type to interact with astronauts, unquote. I told them that I was type O-positive. They wanted someone who was taller, masculine, pinker, and older."

Born in New York, Cowings spent her first twenty-one years in the Fort Apache area of the Bronx. She was the only girl in her family of four

children. For most of her childhood, Cowings' parents owned and oper-
ated a grocery store. "I guess I was closer to my father, because I was the
only girl. We used to talk a lot, and, when I was about nine or ten years
old, I noticed that there seemed to be more opportunities for white people than for black or Hispanic people. And there were more positions
available for men. Every job ended with 'man'—fireman, mailman,
policeman, congressman. I remember going to my father and saying,
'Look, Dad, I just figured this out—black women are at the bottom of
the barrel. What are the opportunities out there for me?' My dad pointed out—and, in retrospect, I believe he influenced what I am today—
that I was a human being, and that human beings were the best damn
animals on the whole damn planet.

"He said that we were made of bone and hair like other animals, but
human beings do miraculous things that some people may think are
commonplace. A human being decided that he wanted to fly, and now we
fly farther than birds. A human being wanted to move about on the
ocean, and he created boats. He wanted to slide down mountains, so he
invented skis. My father bolstered my curiosity, and my curiosity is the
reason I started studying human potential. Even at nine, I was trying to
figure out how I fit into this world."

SELF-ESTEEM, ACHIEVEMENT, AND BLACKNESS

The connection between self-esteem and academic achievement is reasonably well documented. A 1978 study by Leanor B. Johnson on values
in the black family, shows that people like Dr. Cowings—who had a positive self-image as a child—tend toward higher academic and professional achievement than children with low self-esteem. Several
researchers in child development agree that one of the most important
events in the ego development of black children is their recognition of
their blackness and all that it means in a color-conscious society
(Johnson, 1921; Hale-Benson, 1982; David, 1992).

This recognition may come in many forms and at different ages in a
child's life. State Senator Diane Watson, brought up in California, says

that she did not directly experience discrimination or bigotry until she was eighteen years old. It was the 1950s, and she was traveling east on a scholarship to Columbia University. Her awakening came in Fort Knox, Kentucky, while visiting relatives. "We were shopping, and some white guys called me 'nigger.' I was highly insulted and asked, 'Why did they call me a nigger? They don't know me!' That shows how naive I was. I was furious but also reminded where I was."

Author Eloise Greenfield was first traumatized by bigotry as a teenager while riding on a bus in Norfolk, Virginia, during a visit to her grandmother. She wrote about the incident in one of her books, *ChildTimes*. Buses were segregated then in the South. "The bus was crowded," Greenfield recalled, "so I stood near the front. A white man, who appeared intoxicated, said to me, 'You'd better get to the back of the bus.' I looked around and noted that most of the white people appeared embarrassed by his behavior, but they did not come to my defense. Although I moved back, I was embarrassed and felt a rage I will always remember."

Jay David wrote in *Growing Up Black* that when such events happen, a new understanding of self influences the child's every thought and emotion; these events mark the end of innocence for the black child. Suddenly nothing can be taken for granted—a stare, a pat on the head, a casual remark must all be questioned in terms of whether a racial insult or attack has somehow been implied.

Most black families teach their children early in life their own interpretation of the meaning of being black. "Every black child I know," says Harvard child development specialist Robert Coles, "has had to take notice in some way of what skin color signifies in our society." Philanthropist and children's advocate Eileen Norton agrees. She says that she is never unaware that her children look different from other children in the private school they attend.

THE CHALLENGES THAT NEVER DISAPPEAR

Ralph Ellison, author of *The Invisible Man,* once exhorted a group of young black journalists never to accept the stereotype of the black family as broken, just as they must never accept the stereotype of Harlem as "piss in the halls and blood on the stairs." He went on to say that both preconceptions have some basis in reality, but each highly simplifies the complexity of the human condition, denying all that gives black people strength, endurance, and promise.

This strength, endurance, and promise was found in the families of the women I interviewed. "Those with self-esteem will not let anything or anyone prevent them from climbing toward their goal," Dr. Lydia Pettis-Patton told me. "I don't care what environment they are raised in, be it an impoverished environment like mine or in a single-parent situation in an illiterate family environment or one where the child has middle-class parents with middle-class values. I grew up poor in a segregated environment. Until I was seventeen, I ventured no more than forty miles from Fort Lauderdale. I did not have the advantage of travel to develop my self-esteem or knowledge of the world. My concept of self developed within my surroundings. My desire to achieve and the positive feelings I have about myself helped me overcome all barriers that researchers say are responsible for failure in the underclass."

Bishop Leontine Kelly and publisher Ruth Washington both expressed great concern about the lack of self-affirmation for black children. "A part of growing up must be in knowing that certain things are expected of you," Bishop Kelly told me. "I think part of our legacy was lost in the process of integration. There is also that sense of knowing that you can be more than what anybody says or expects of you. I think we have lost a great deal of wanting to be more than is expected of us. Very little is expected of youth these days, especially black youth. Many of our children are not performing within the parameters of higher expectations."

"Unfortunately," Ruth Washington told me before she died, "the significance of the color of one's skin continues to be a challenge for black Americans. In addition to the tremendous toll it takes on the welfare and well-being of little black children, the difficulties facing the black family in helping their young children cope in our society can be frustrating and intricate."

Reverend Ella Mitchell remembers her upbringing as being completely different from that of today's children. "My parents tried to protect us from the evils of segregation and bigotry as best they could. Although we lived in a white neighborhood, there still existed the tradition of black and white separation. White children went to white schools, and black children went to black ones. In my community there was a subtle type of intolerance that harmed the esteem of young black girls. White families thought that when black girls became a certain age, they were a sexual threat to their young males. That tradition has been permanently etched in my consciousness; it was a sad indignity that all black girls experienced when they came of age. While we were youngsters, we could visit the homes of our white neighbors and play with their children. Then, as we entered adolescence, we were no longer welcome in their homes and were told, "Sorry, this is it." It certainly wasn't because our families failed to teach values and ethics in our homes. My mother was probably more strict than any other mother in the community. I know that she was more strict than my father, who was a minister. She grew up in a strict environment, so she knew no other way."

Eloise Greenfield comments, "I think self-esteem has to come first. If self-esteem and confidence are present at the beginning, we are challenged to take risks. We can try different things without the need to test our self-worth. So, when I was testing myself to see if I could write, I was not testing my personal worth; I was testing to see if I had the skills and talent to become a writer.

"I think one of the most wonderful gifts I received from my parents was that they never said, 'You have to be at the top.' In other words, they were saying to me that I was already worthy. I did not need to make a space in this world, because I already had the space. They encouraged me without requiring that I prove something. I had nothing to prove, so it gave me freedom to do what I wanted to do and to be what I wanted to be."

When businesswoman Zelma Stennis was asked about self-esteem, she replied: "I always felt different. I didn't feel that I was where I belonged—I belonged somewhere else. Also, I cannot say that I felt beautiful, but I felt special. I'd look in the mirror and I did not see on the outside what I felt on the inside. I kept trying to figure out what to do with myself. My dream was to become a concert pianist, but my family could not afford to support my dreams, and the act of finding a sponsor was out of the question for a little black girl growing up in Detroit. But things did happen to confirm that I was special. I have saved, to this day, a newspaper clipping of me standing with singer Marian Anderson. I was selected to present her with a citation, which was a real honor. Although one may consider my life a success, I still have dreams, nightmares, and fantasies. I still have a burning flame deep within me that refuses to go out. Even now I feel that there are so many things that need to be done, and I wish I were capable of doing them."

State Senator Diane Watson recalls that being black was a badge her family wore proudly. "My family was goal directed. We made our own opportunities. We did not have a lot of money, but we had good role models, wise advice, and family unity. I came from a matriarchal family. My grandmother and her sister, Pauline Slater, were two very strong people." Watson's maternal grandmother, Belle O'Neal, was educated in the field of nursing. She assisted in the first open heart surgery in Chicago. O'Neal and her sister Pauline were the first in their family to be college educated. "My aunt Pauline is a legend in this town [Los Angeles] and was my very first role model and mentor. She was the first person I ever knew with three master's degrees—one from Cambridge University, England. When the Los Angeles school board decided to hire its first black teacher, they chose Pauline Slater. Her brother, Duke Slater, was an All-American at Iowa State at Clinton and later became a judge in Chicago."

Childhood experiences gave investment banker Iris Rideau the motivation to succeed. "When I was ten years old, I convinced my mother to move to Los Angeles. I was hoping for a reconciliation between my parents, since my father had left Chicago and purchased a ranch near Los Angeles. Before we moved to California, I traveled from New Orleans each summer to spend time with my father. Life with him was different from my life in New Orleans. I moved between two lifestyles, one financially wanting and the other affluent. I liked what the affluent one provided; I was delighted with California. My father, who had become a successful entrepreneur, bought things like ranches and markets—anything that would return a profit.

"He took me places and bought me pretty clothes from Bullocks Wilshire and Saks Fifth Avenue in Beverly Hills. He gave me a glimpse of what I wanted in my life. It was the kind of life I wanted for myself, but when I returned home to New Orleans life was different . . . I became quite confused. That was the beginning of my determination never to be poor again."

Motivational speaker and fashion historian Kaycee Hale says, "I marvel at the miracle of life and stand in awe of its perfection . . . The body is a vehicle. Most of us spend a great deal of time worrying about how the outside package looks . . . The facade seems more important than what is inside. This packaging is only important because of the value society places on looks. To me, the inner self is the essence of our being . . . The development of self-esteem and confidence is so very important. If we could just get our mind, spirit, and body in motion with the rhythm and harmony of the universe, what an incredible world this could be."

CRYING ON THE INSIDE, SMILING ON THE OUTSIDE

Historically—and, sadly, even today—skin color has cast a shadow over the lives of many black children. From an early age, they will have heard some variation of the adage, "White is right; if you're brown, stick around; if you're black, get back." These cruel words are spoken not only by white children to black children, but also by black children to their peers.

I did not expect actress Donzaleigh Abernathy to have felt rejection because of her skin color when she was growing up; after all, she is exceptionally attractive and also the daughter of Reverend Ralph D.

Abernathy, the highly regarded civil rights leader and associate of Dr. Martin Luther King, Jr. As I listened to her describe her pain, it brought into focus for me what other brown-skinned African Americans have felt but are loath to discuss publicly. Abernathy remembers one day when she was a little girl: "Andrew Young, the former Ambassador to the United Nations and Atlanta's former mayor, told me a story of the ugly duckling that turned into a swan. I was crying because some kids in my neighborhood, who were lighter than I, had made fun of the color of my skin, and Andrew Young told me the story to cheer me up. It made me feel good. I said to myself, 'One day I am going to be a swan.' I was a cute little girl, but I felt so ugly because I was told that my brown skin was ugly. Years later, just before my wedding, I saw Andy and he said, 'Where did you get the audacity to turn out so beautiful?' I said, 'I'm the ugly duckling that turned into a swan.' He had given me hope so many years before. As long as you have that hope, you can learn to love yourself. If you love yourself, other people will love you. I stopped being ashamed of myself a long time ago . . .

"Most roles written for black women are usually 'street roles,' and I don't fit into that stereotype. Black filmmakers, unfortunately, help to perpetuate that image. When they look for a beautiful black woman, she has to be fair-skinned, have straight hair, and be tall. They don't seem to understand that beauty comes in all shapes, sizes, and colors. I believe that if we are to elevate the self-esteem of black youth and the black race, we have to show beautiful women who are brown, dark brown, as well as fair. And not say, by way of films, that the yellow, Nordic-looking black woman is what we consider beautiful and who we aspire to be. Our beauty comes in a rainbow of colors.

"I long for the day when there are more faces on the movie screen and on television that little black girls can identify with, and say, 'Wow, she looks like me. I can look like that, she's pretty, she's strong, and she's smart.'

From my own childhood days at an all-black school in Houston, I have vivid and haunting memories of three very light-skinned sisters whose family name, appropriately enough, was *Snow.* As long as I was at

Jack Yates High, one of the Snow girls marched in front of the band as the drum major. No other girl had a chance as long as at least one of the Snow sisters was enrolled. The dean of girls, Mrs. O'Neal, made sure that the baton was passed on from Snow to Snow. Dean O'Neal was also nearly white—with stringy, dirty-brown, thin, straight hair worn in a bun at the nape of her neck—and as color-conscious as any racist Boer in old South Africa. We other girls could be drum majorettes, lead the girls' pep squad, or be cheerleaders, but we could never hope to wear the tall, white, furry drum major's hat or carry the long, slender baton with the big, shiny ball on top. That represented the crown and scepter of the Snow queens.

Dean O'Neal was not the only African American who promoted this type of discrimination. Some blacks have helped to perpetuate the American version of apartheid. During my college days, there were Greek-letter sororities at some black colleges that chose only near-white female students. We have not come too far from the time, in the '30s and '40s, when Catholic schools in some Louisiana parishes admitted little children according to a "paper bag" test. If you were as light or lighter than a paper bag, you could go to certain Catholic schools; if darker, you were turned away. At several private black colleges in the South, a photograph had to accompany each application. These schools chose only "appropriate" applicants. Such practices are illegal now in the United States—or at least for the moment they're still illegal.

A DIVISIVE LEGACY

Skin color has been an issue in this country since the first white people set foot on these shores from Europe. With the beginning of slavery, when the first child with the blood of a black slave and a white plantation owner or overseer was born, the issue of race and color in America became even more complicated. With the South being a close-knit society, the lives of blacks and whites could not help but become intertwined and intermingled.

The rape of female slaves by white men and the congress between female slaves or Indian women with Spanish and French settlers—especially in the Louisiana Territory—diversified the the racial gene pool. This is evidenced by the infinite variety of types and colors among black people in the United States today. Although marriages between blacks and whites were forbidden in the old South, marriages between blacks and Indians were not uncommon, especially in the Oklahoma territory.

Donzaleigh Abernathy told me, "My great-grandfather was a full-blooded Native American. As a child, especially when she saw me crying, my grandmother—three-quarters Indian—would tell me, 'You're an Indian woman. Indian women don't cry.'"

For the female slave, the sexual association with her master was apt to bring favors and possibly freedom for herself and her children. These "chosen" slaves and their offspring became the privileged house servants and artisans, giving rise to a caste system among slaves that remains in the consciousness of many blacks and whites even today.

Mixed-race slaves quickly separated into an in-between class that enjoyed higher social status than the darker-hued slaves. And yet, more often than not, a slave-owner would grant freedom only to his mixed-black family upon his death, if at all. Thomas Jefferson, for instance, instructed his legitimate daughter to free his black mistress, Sally Hemings, and her children after he died.

The power of this caste system among blacks only recently began to diminish, when the law mandated greater opportunities for all people to participate in the benefits of the social and economic system in this country, regardless of race or color. As I interviewed African American women for this book, I found myself face-to-face with the curious and seemingly absurd question, "What is a black American?"

During my interview with investment broker Iris Rideau, she noted, "I was raised in a complicated family environment. We were called Creoles because we had a mixture of a little African American and a lot of Spanish and French. We had our own communities and our own language, which is a mixture of French and English. We had a lot of pride about ourselves as a group. Although many Creole families kept to themselves, I mixed with everybody. We were considered black, just as other

African Americans were. Some in our families were blondes with blue eyes, but they still were considered black. We had no special privileges outside our community. Being born in the South, all black people experienced the pains of prejudice."

In one of her addresses, Dr. Mary McLeod Bethune quoted a plea by Frederick Douglass, in which he asked that Negroes not be judged by the heights to which they have risen, but by the depths from which they have climbed. Judged on that basis, Bethune said, the black woman embodies one of the modern miracles of the nation. Certainly the women I interviewed can all be seen as examples of this miracle. With the help of family and community, these women refused to let anything be a hindrance to their participation in the American dream. Despite the tremendous toll that racism could have taken on them, they emerged confident, self-assured, and fiercely determined to fulfill their most cherished goals. They had extensive family support and good internalized control through parental discipline; they developed a healthy sense of personal power stemming from high self-esteem and pride in their identity as black Americans.

PART II

THE LIGHT THAT WON'T GO OUT

Every woman has a right to be all that she can be,
and to know all she can know.

—ANONYMOUS

CHAPTER 4

EDUCATION AS A TOOL

*"I did not want to be a doctor like my father, but . . . I enjoyed
science . . . When I was a child, I used to mix solutions together
and put them under the bathtub, and let the mixture set for weeks
to see what the results were."*   —JEWEL PLUMMER COBB, PH.D.

AFTER FINISHING HIGH SCHOOL in Chicago, Jewel Plummer
Cobb went directly to the University of Michigan at Ann Arbor,
where she spent three semesters. "It was a perfect example of
Northern segregation in the forties," she told me. "We were not allowed
to live in the campus dormitories unless we could pass for white. There
was one black female student who lived in the women's dorm—the university officials did not know that she was black. Three young black men
lived in the men's dorm, mainly because one of them was the son of a
state senator."

Besides being forced to live in segregated housing, black students at
Ann Arbor were not allowed to go for beer at the Pretzel House, the pub
where all the white students went after the games. Class size was also very
large, making it even harder to make friends. Although Cobb says that
she enjoyed her time at the University of Michigan, she and her parents
decided that at Talladega College, a black college in Alabama, she would
enjoy a better life. "After I received my B.S. degree from Talladega, I

entered New York University, where I received a master's and a Ph.D. I was awarded a teaching fellowship at the university and received a post-doctoral fellowship from the National Cancer Institute to conduct research at Harlem Hospital and Columbia University."

Cobb worked for two years at the Harlem Hospital Research Foundation as a researcher in biology, funded by grants from the National Cancer Institute. While at Harlem Hospital she accepted an opportunity to return to Chicago to teach in the anatomy department at the University of Illinois Medical School. While there, she continued her cancer research. "After two years, I left the university because I married a man from New York . . . I rejoined the Cancer Research Foundation, which by then had moved from Harlem Hospital to New York University Medical School, where I conducted research for [the next] six years.

"I had to make a choice between the long hours required for my research and my family—by then my son was born. I had taught for five years during my graduate fellowship days at the university, and I liked teaching, so I decided to return to a college environment." Cobb went on to accept teaching and administrative posts at Sarah Lawrence College and Connecticut College before accepting the position of president of California State University at Fullerton.

Now retired, Cobb remains active in the university community as a trustee professor. "My dream is to continue to make inroads into the problems of underrepresentation of minorities in education." She is particularly concerned about minorities and women in science and is an avid supporter of Quality Education for Minorities (QEM), based in Washington, D.C., which addresses this issue on a national level.

"IF YOU DON'T HAVE AN EDUCATION. . ."

The majority of black people throughout American history have treated education as their holy grail. Like Booker T. Washington, who believed that an ambitious mind will seize upon education as the key to success and power, black parents have held tenaciously to the belief that the lives of their children can be improved by education.

For the parents of Linda Carol Brown in Topeka, Kansas, that belief was strong enough to inspire landmark legislation creating equal educational opportunity for children of all races in our country. Linda's parents felt that it made no sense for their eight-year-old daughter to walk twenty-one blocks to an inferior school when a better school was just five blocks away—notwithstanding that the superior school had never admitted a black child to its student body. Mr. Brown sued the Topeka Board of Education. On May 17, 1954, the United States Supreme Court untied what Chief Justice Earl Warren called the longstanding "Gordian knot of educational deceit." *Brown vs. The Board of Education* broke the back of legal apartheid in the school systems of the nation and served as the cornerstone that has supported all of our subsequent civil rights legislation, ultimately touching every aspect of American life—not only in education, but also in jobs, housing, and equal access to restaurants and clubs, and equal access and equal opportunity for women and gays.

Before that historical moment, education had been hard to come by for African Americans. There were laws in the South that forbade the education of blacks, even free blacks. In 1853, in Norfolk, Virginia, one Margaret Douglass was arrested for teaching in a school attended by free Negro children, having committed an offense "against the peace and dignity of the Commonwealth of Virginia" (quoted in a 1921 article by William Seneca Sutton in Julia Johnson's book, *The Negro Program*). Douglass was tried, convicted, and sentenced to 30 days' imprisonment— a punishment that the trial judge declared was to "serve as a terror to those who acknowledged no rule of action except their own evil will and pleasure." Virtually all of the parents of the thirty-two women profiled here felt as strongly about quality education for their children as did the parents of Linda Carol Brown. The attitude of this earlier generation is reflected in the words of Bishop Leontine Kelly: "If we are educated, we are more apt to be accepted in society. We, of course, know that education does not assure acceptance, but at least it is an important step."

Pat Cowings told me, "As long as it was for education, my parents would do anything. They felt that if you were going to achieve, you had to have a proper background; and that background . . . was education."

The children in the Cowings family were achievers. Pat Cowings and one of her brothers attended New York's High School of Music and Arts, a highly acclaimed and selective arts school. The other two brothers attended the Bronx High School of Science, which had a comparable program devoted to the sciences. "My parents fostered in us good study habits. They saw to it that we did our very best in school. My mother read to us, and later encouraged us to read . . . My father was very strict about our study habits. We had to spend a specific time each day with homework. We would either sit in the phone booth in the grocery store that we owned, so he could see us studying, or we would sit in the back of the car, which was parked in front of the store, and study by the street-lights. We were rewarded for our efforts with *As* on our report cards . . . My aunt had a doctorate in psychology from Columbia. I pretty much decided when I was a teenager that I wanted to be a psychologist."

An avid reader of science fiction and a *Star Trek* fan, Cowings managed to talk her way into a graduate course on space shuttle technology at UC Davis that had formerly been restricted to students with a bachelor of science degree in engineering. "I discovered that the space program faced a number of biomedical problems that did not seem solvable by conventional medical techniques. So I wrote a paper—a requirement for the course—on the applications of autogenic-feedback training, the process of conditioning people to consciously control their own bodily responses. The application for this treatment involved about twelve different biological problems experienced on extended manned space flights. I got an *A* for the paper. In the same course, we went on a class trip . . . I discovered NASA, and was hooked."

SEGREGATED SCHOOLS IN THE SOUTH

As I spoke with women around the country, I watched for an educational success theme that might develop around the experiences of the women who grew up in the South as compared to women from other areas. What emerged was both disturbing and fascinating: The majority of the southern women felt comfortable, protected, and secure in their segregated environments, and, if anything, seemed to do better for having been set apart. Despite inferior school facilities, worn textbooks, and out-of-date equipment, the parents and teachers of these girls were able to help them develop a positive attitude and healthy self-esteem and to attain the best education possible within an underfunded and under-privileged school system.

Leisure Services general manager Dr. Lydia Pettis-Patton called my attention to the fact that she grew up in all-black elementary and high schools during the fifties. "All my early school experiences were in total-ly black settings. I never had a white teacher or came into contact with whites during my school years. Although whites lived in the community and I knew how to relate to them, they were never a part of my immedi-ate environment. I was nurtured and supported and competed within a positive black environment and was allowed to develop within that environment. So when I left my community to go to college, which I did straight out of high school, I had to prove myself. I had achieved in my black environment, and I wanted everybody to know—when competing with whites in college—that I was good at whatever I did. So I focused on what to me was a huge concern—that was to get the opposite race to take me seriously, to accept my talent and abilities, and not to restrict me because of my color."

Pettis-Patton says that her biggest educational challenge was "fight-ing for my Ph.D." She was the only black female accepted into her pro-gram's class of eighteen doctoral students at Virginia Commonwealth University. "Very early in the program, we chose our chairperson and the others on our doctoral committee. I did fine in the coursework, making *As* and an occasional *B*. After I finished my coursework and was ready to submit my doctoral proposal, the committee's attitudes appeared to change . . . [They] finally realized that I would soon have that presti-gious Ph.D. 'calling card' they possessed. Being white Ph.D.s, they could not conceive that a black woman would soon be one also. About the time I presented my doctoral proposal, the games started: 'How many hurdles must she go through in order to get that piece of paper?' I really had to jump over high hurdles. After I presented my proposal and was about to start writing the dissertation, my chairperson told me that she would not entertain the thought of my taking less than two years to write my [thesis]. I told her that I planned to complete my dissertation in one year and walk across that stage on May 17, 1986. She was talking about 1987, so it became very clear that we were on two different timelines."

After that meeting, Pettis-Patton made a request to change chairpersons. She was told by the director of the program that her request could not be honored. "It was difficult, but I did get another chairperson, a black female, Dr. Daisy Reid, who was very supportive and understanding, but did not make the way easy for me. She did, however, stand up for me when she felt the rest of the committee was harassing me. With the support from my husband, the grace of God, and the guidance from Dr. Reid, I received my Ph.D. on May 17, 1986, within my scheduled timeframe."

Like Pettis-Patton, Vivian Pinn, assistant director of women's health at The National Institutes of Health in Washington, D.C., grew up in a segregated community and attended segregated schools. Her senior class at Dunbar High in Lynchburg, Virginia, was the first class, following the desegregation of schools in the South, permitted to take the national college entrance exams.

After graduating from high school as valedictorian, Pinn was admitted to Wellesley, a highly regarded women's college in Massachusetts. "I didn't know what to expect. I knew that I was going to an excellent school. I, of course, expected to work hard at whatever school I attended. But having come from a segregated school in the South, it was quite a challenge to compete with the best students from across the country.

"What got me through Wellesley was the self-discipline I learned at home and at school. Although my high school was segregated, we had excellent teachers who encouraged excellence from the students. My teachers taught me how to study, while my parents taught me the meaning of hard work. My parents also helped me develop a willingness to be able to sacrifice certain pleasures in order to succeed in my studies."

Pinn says the environment at Wellesley was stimulating because of the presence of so many bright, enthusiastic, motivated, and competitive young women. "You'd find yourself saying, 'I'm going to do it, too. I'm going to survive. I'm going to give it my all.' And I did. I gave it my all and succeeded. Wellesley was also a nurturing environment where the faculty and staff took time to listen to us students and to assist us, although no one there was going to take us by the hand and lead us. The academic and cultural exposure at Wellesley was first class. I enjoyed it and worked hard. I did not have much time for a social life. I was one of four black women in my class of about 465 students. Because I came from a segregated school, I felt that I had to work harder. I had not enjoyed many of the opportunities that the white students had experienced. However, I feel that I received an excellent education at Wellesley. The school prepared me to face all future challenges with confidence."

After she received her bachelor's degree, Pinn returned to Virginia to enroll in the School of Medicine at the University of Virginia, where she was the only black and the only woman in her class. Unlike other black students at the university, Pinn did not have problems with discrimination while she attended medical school. "Discrimination and racial attitudes did not affect me as traumatically as they did others who were not from the South. Since I had grown up in Virginia, I was familiar with its tradition, even though I had spent a few years in the North.

"On the other hand, in medical school, you either hung in there or got lost," Pinn reports. "I survived the rigors of medical school because I could not disappoint my father or mother, who saw me enter Wellesley but, because of her death, my mother did not get to see me become a doctor. Both my parents were important to the successful completion of my dream . . . [W]hen I was four years old, I told them that I wanted to be a pediatrician. Although I chose pathology instead, my family supported my efforts to accomplish my goal."

Reverend Ella Mitchell's father and mother, like so many of the parents of the women profiled here, were well educated. Her father received a bachelor's degree in 1900 and a seminary degree in 1903, from Biddle University in Charlotte, North Carolina—now Johnson C. Smith University. "My father had two master's degrees. Mother graduated from Avery Institute in Charleston and taught school for many years there.

Later she worked for the Boy's Club in Charleston. This was odd, since she had no boys at home.

"It was important to my parents that their children receive an excellent education. My sisters, Jess and Ermine, and my cousin, Beulah, went to private schools in another city. My parents thought that the girls would be better educated and develop better social skills if they attended school in a controlled environment. By the time I reached high school, Charleston had improved its education for black students, so I stayed home and went to Miss Missy Sanders School, and later to Avery Institute, the school my mother graduated from earlier."

When Mitchell graduated from high school at age seventeen, three of her teachers at Avery encouraged her to attend their alma mater, Talladega College in Alabama. "These teachers thought Talladega was an excellent school, and I agree. When I first entered, I wanted to major in religion, but that was not possible. There were not enough professors to create a religion department. Instead, I began a major in sociology, and later transferred to religion when that department increased its staff.

"After graduating and working a few years, I left the South for New York City, where I was accepted at the Union Theological Seminary. My first application was to Yale University. Yale wrote back that they had no fieldwork for women, especially for black women. Yale suggested that I apply to Union, which I did. I was in seminary in 1941, which accounts for the fact that we had so few women. Hardly anybody at that time expected a black woman to go to seminary. I studied under such notable professors as Paul Tillich, Reinhold Niebuhr, Harry Emerson Fosdyck, George Buttrick, Mary Ely Lyman, and Sophia Lyons Fahs—all top theologians. I was the second black woman to graduate from Union Theological Seminary. Eunice Jackson, who was graduated in 1938, became the first black woman to be accepted and graduated. Union was where I met my husband, Reverend Dr. Henry H. Mitchell. When he asked me to marry him, he reminded me that we were working toward the same goals, so why not work together?" Although Mitchell was the second African American woman to graduate from Union Theological Seminary, she was the first to get her doctorate, in 1974, at the highly respected Claremont School of Theology in Claremont, California.

Kaycee Hale, a fashion model, motivational speaker, and founder-developer of the world's largest network of educationally affiliated fashion research centers, grew up in another sort of environment altogether. "In Mount Hope, West Virginia," she told me, "there was no need for formal education." When you meet Kaycee Hale, it's hard to believe that this sophisticated and elegant woman grew up in the back woods of West Virginia among coal miners.

Hale spent her childhood and teenage years in the small, parochial town of Mount Hope, population 6,000. Here hardworking, poorly paid black families had little control over their economic or educational lives, and, except for the black church, few opportunities for a quality life. The only book in Hale's home was the Bible, and conversation revolved around the family's day-to-day existence. No one in Hale's family had an education beyond high school, so it was not surprising that Hale had no awareness of college as a possibility, much less something to strive for.

From early childhood until she graduated from high school at age seventeen, Hale lived with her grandparents. "Mama, my grandmother, had a third-grade education, and she could neither read nor write well. I have strong memories of coming home one afternoon and showing Mama my report card. When she read it and was about to sign it, I noticed that she looked sort of agitated, so I asked her what was wrong. She said, 'Well Honey, we have to talk.' She sat me down and said, 'This grade card means that you are going into the fourth grade. I don't know what they teach in the fourth grade. I can't help you anymore. You will have to go on your own.' While she talked to me, I noticed tears in her eyes. She thought that she had nothing else to contribute toward my education. But she was wrong. Mama was strong. Although she did not have much schooling, she had native intelligence. You see, Mama was from Virginia, where education for blacks was not encouraged. Her mother died when she was nine, so she had to work in the fields, and that was when her formal education stopped."

Although Hale's grandmother was unaware of opportunities for blacks outside her limited environs, she wanted her granddaughter to have a better life than she had. "Mama used to tell me that she wanted me to do whatever it took, and she would do whatever she could do, to free me from the exploitive, slavelike world my family lived in around the coalmines. She did not want me washing another woman's underwear. When Mama was a maid, she had to wash Mrs. Stroke's underwear—by hand.

"Mama was a short woman, about four feet, eleven inches tall, and she weighed about a hundred eighty pounds. She was tremendously heavy, but she had a genuine homespun love and passion for life. She thought her deep faith in God gave her the inborn mother-wit to know how to achieve the possible, and sometimes the impossible. I can't imagine having achieved anything without the foundation that she helped me build.

"My grandfather had gone through the second grade, and my father finished tenth grade. When I was there, West Virginia had one of the worst educational systems in the United States, ranking number forty-eight in the forty-eight states. Just being there made a black child underprivileged. Mama thought it was absolutely wonderful that I finished elementary school. When I graduated from junior high school with honors, to her every step of the way was a great accomplishment. It was God's will."

Hale was nine years old before she ever saw a library—actually it was a bookmobile. No one in her neighborhood had ever seen anything like it. This was the middle '50s, when some of the opportunities of the New South were emerging. Curious to see the inside of the big bus-type vehicle people called a bookmobile, Hale carefully made her way up the steps and into a brand-new, brightly lit world of shelves filled with books. She was at first surprised, then fascinated to see books that were not marked-up and worn like the ones at school. From that day on, the bookmobile was her sanctuary, where she absorbed knowledge and ideas like a sponge. "I entered a new world of learning, helped along by a gracious, warm, and friendly librarian, Mrs. Maude A. Roby. We developed a friendship that helped change my life. Between Mama and Mrs. Roby, I developed a thirst for learning that has not been quenched. Perhaps that is why I chose libraries after graduating and moving to Los Angeles to live with my parents. When I left Mount Hope, my whole life changed. Los Angeles became my mecca for both educational and career opportunities."

INTEGRATED SCHOOLS AND THEIR FOIBLES

Unlike the women who grew up in segregated schools, most of the women who went to integrated schools were made aware of their racial differences at an early age. Businesswoman Zelma Stennis describes an experience during her high school years in Detroit. Highly talented in music, she wanted to learn a variety of musical instruments available to students at the school. One of the instruments that appealed to Stennis was the harp. "To take harp lessons and be a part of the harp ensemble was one of my high school dreams . . . [T]here were only ten in the ensemble . . . The harp teacher felt that you had to be an angel to play a harp—to have the looks, the carriage, and the voice. I seemed never to measure up to what she required, although I was an accomplished musician. However, I was persistent and kept going back, until finally she said, 'Zelma, you can audition tomorrow in front of the assembly.' She thought I would back out, because two hundred or more kids would be in the audience looking at me play. It was frightening, but I did it, and she had to admit me into the harpists' hallowed halls—nine blond girls with blue eyes, who looked like the teacher's concept of angelhood, and Zelma."

Stennis remembers attitudes toward education in the neighborhood where she grew up. "Some could afford to give their children a college education, but most could not. My father was not able to send us to college, but he promised each of us eight children a high school education." Determined to further her education as a classical pianist, Stennis enrolled concurrently at Wayne State University and the Detroit Conservatory of Music. She worked two and three part-time jobs to get money for her tuition and music lessons. One of her part-time jobs was giving piano lessons to the children in the community. "I would have my own piano lesson, and then get on the bus and return to my neighborhood to give a piano lesson to one of the children. Sometimes the mothers couldn't pay me. They were poor people, the same as most families in our community. I would get home from the university around ten o'clock at night and would study in the kitchen because the family was asleep. Sometimes I was so tired I fell asleep, wrapped in a blanket to keep warm, with a book in front of me. I never felt I was putting the effort in my college work the way I could have because of the pressures of work. I still have [the desire] to be on a campus and do nothing but study. That must be a wonderful feeling."

Terri Wright maintained good grades in school and knew that she would go to college. "I have always done well in an academic environment. Since early on, I was goal directed. My parents were proud people; although neither was highly educated, they respected education and believed that it was necessary for the accomplishment of goals. Two of my mother's siblings pursued higher degrees. My uncle is a college professor in Jamaica, and my aunt, Dr. Joyce Craft, is a principal with the Los Angeles Unified School District.

"I think my biggest disappointment came when it was time to apply to a college. I had always assumed that I would go to the college of my choice, and my expenses would be paid by my family. I had not realized that the family budget did not include money for college. When my friends were applying to prestigious schools such as Princeton, Harvard, and Mount Holyoke, it suddenly dawned on me that I could not afford to apply to these schools. It was a real let-down. If I were going to go to college, I would have to remain in New York and attend school there. The college system was free at that time."

Wright attended York College in the Jamaica-Queens area of New York City. "For a while I lived at home, but later moved into my own apartment near the family home in Queens. My family helped me financially and regularly brought me 'care packages.' I worked full-time during college and sometimes carried eighteen units. When people say that they can't work full-time and take a full schedule at school, I don't want to hear it. If you want it bad enough, you can do it.

"I enjoyed college. I went to a wonderful school. York was in an area that, at the time, bordered the ghetto. The college had a real sense of community and a sense of responsibility to the community. There were professors who cared, and the curriculum was oriented toward hands-on learning in the community. I knew that I wanted to work in school and community health, and York College offered me the opportunity to train in that field.

"It was during the time I worked at Planned Parenthood that I decided to return to school to obtain my master's degree. I applied to the five top schools in the country that offered advanced degrees in public health. It became quite clear to me by then that when black people pursue a particular field of study, they have to seek out the best schools. The people in authority look at that piece of paper in terms of where it's from. Of course, it's important for everyone, but especially for minorities. Certainly an MBA from Harvard has more status than one from Georgia State. Your credentials are especially scrutinized when you are a person of color."

Wright applied to the schools of public health at Harvard, Columbia, the University of Michigan, the University of California at Berkeley, and the University of North Carolina at Chapel Hill. "I was accepted at Columbia but was not offered a scholarship. Harvard returned my application because they required a second professional degree, such as a medical, a dental, or a law degree. The University of Michigan accepted me and offered me a full scholarship. If I had not gotten into one of those schools, I would not have returned to school until one of them accepted me. Now I am considering another degree, and if I don't get into one of the top schools in the nation, I will not go."

In the 1940s, when Mary Jane Hewitt was growing up in St. Paul, Minnesota, black families were in the minority there. "Although there were no posted signs of discrimination, it existed. My mother told us never to allow the barriers of racism that existed then to keep us from preparing for a brighter future. She had a strong belief that you made advancement through education. We girls were told that there was more in this world for a woman than being a homemaker. Not that homemaking was unimportant; but if you chose to pursue a career outside the home, you should have an opportunity to do so."

Most of Hewitt's classmates were first-generation Americans. "The same thing that was being pounded into my head was being pounded into the heads of every child in my community: 'The way you can advance is through education.' Nobody ever questioned that maxim. It was the norm in my community. You also competed for the best grades. In fact, you were perceived as an oddball if you did not achieve. At home your parents encouraged you, and you were punished for infractions. You were motivated in school. Teachers took an interest in you. You were praised for what you accomplished. You got recognition for your achievements. You got it from all sides—from your parents, your teachers, and your community. So I can't imagine a kid growing up in that community not achieving and not having a positive concept of themselves. That was what it was all about."

Hewitt's educational achievements include a bachelor's degree from the University of Minnesota and a master's degree and a Ph.D. in English and comparative literature from the University of the West Indies. "I chose the University of the West Indies for my studies for two reasons. First, as a minority growing up in this country, I wanted to feel a part of the majority for a change. The University of the West Indies was the only Caribbean institution that had survived the attempts at federation by the former British colonies. It was based on the British system where one could do a research degree and choose the course work that related to one's research. I felt that was for me."

Hewitt's doctoral thesis was a comparative study of two African Diaspora women writers, Zora Neale Hurston and Louise Bennett, one from the United States and one from Jamaica. "Zora Neale Hurston, many Americans know about; the other, Louise Bennett—a folklorist, performer, social commentator, and 'nation language' poet—is called the cultural bank of Jamaica.

"If Hurston had lived in another time and another place, she would have had a successful life. She had her fifteen minutes of fame, and then it was gone. This very talented, Renaissance woman died alone, a pauper, very disappointed and frustrated in a welfare house in St. Lucie County, Florida. It was tragic. I believe that it was Terence, the Roman playwright, who said, 'Geography is Fate.' The time of birth is also fate. It is not only geography; it is the time we are born."

NEVER TOO LATE TO RETURN

While the majority of women I interviewed went directly to college after high school, a few returned to school only later in life. The experience of Doris Topsy-Elvord, the first woman elected to the city council in Long Beach, California, is an example of the hardships that many women have faced when they've wanted to better their lot by returning to school. Topsy-Elvord's husband believed that her place was in their home rearing their three sons. Even though she was willing to work two part-time jobs in order to be with her children when they arrived home from school, her husband was not willing to acknowledge her aspirations. "My husband put many obstacles in my way. He, of course, refused to help me with the housework or the children and made it as difficult as possible for me to get an education. It was a sheer struggle all the way, but I was determined to make it. Then a most incredible thing happened a few weeks before my graduation: In order to qualify for my degree, I wrote several term papers. I had spent hours in the library doing research and many hours writing the papers. One evening when I returned home from work, I found all my beautiful work destroyed. My husband had not only burned the papers that I had worked so hard on, but he had burned all my books. I was devastated. What could I do? I did the only thing I could possibly do—I talked to my professors and explained to them what happened. They loaned me their books and allowed me to reconstruct the papers. I was able to do that and graduated from college with a 3.9 grade point average. I went on to earn a master's degree from Chapman College, where my grade point average was 4.0. I received the admiration of my sons, who have gone on to get their college degrees, and I divorced their father.

"I don't want to give a picture of a husband who was generally mean-spirited. In many ways, he was a good husband and father. We remained friends after the divorce, and he continued to be a good father. In fact he lived about six blocks down the street from us. Before he died in 1986, we were all there for him, including my new husband, Ralph."

Ambassador Cynthia Shepard Perry's husband accepted the fact that she would return to school to complete her bachelor's and get a master's degree, but he did not want her getting a Ph.D. "Most of the parents in my community had little education," recalled Perry, "but held it in high regard. I graduated from high school when I was seventeen and entered Indiana University soon after. I left college in my freshman year, which disappointed my parents. You see, I fell in love and was married before my eighteenth birthday." Although she was anxious to return to college, Perry and her first husband agreed that she would not return until after the children were in school. "When my oldest child was seven, I prepared to return to the university, but discovered that I was pregnant with our fourth child. Finally, nine years after my initial entrance into the university, I returned to school.

"When I returned, my husband did not complain. He also did not complain when I received my master's degree. It was when I told him that I was giving up my job at IBM and returning to school for my doctorate that the stuff hit the fan. He said he wanted a divorce. I didn't know if he was serious or not."

Perry's husband felt that it was a "Ph.D or me." She chose the Ph.D., because getting her degree was an important step toward her ultimate goal of becoming an ambassador. Her husband thought she had enough education, and that it was time for her to concentrate on the children's education. She learned that his friends were laughing at him: He couldn't deal with Perry's having more education than he had.

Aleta Carpenter was initially uninterested in college; she got married the day after her high school prom. "When I first married, I watched soap operas all day and worked in my garden. My first child, Krystal, and I often met my husband at the bus and walked home with him to a dinner waiting on the stove." Her husband was a college graduate who worked as a bacteriologist. "My life revolved around my husband and my child.

For the first year, being housewife and mother sufficed, but I soon knew that I could not continue to watch soap operas and read magazines and books all day and meet my husband at the bus stop in the evening." Carpenter realized that getting a college education would be an important step toward achieving personal fulfillment and satisfaction in her life.

An unmotivated student in high school, Carpenter had received As only in a few favorite classes. Later, when she enrolled in a community college, her grades improved. "I would like to take credit for getting good grades in junior college, but the school I attended did not require much from the students. However, things were different at California State University at Hayward, where I earned my B.A. in sociology and criminal justice. There I had a rude awakening: I had to work hard to get good grades. I performed well in classes such as criminal and contract law and struggled in classes which dealt with torts and math.

"I had wanted to be a probation officer since I was twelve years old. Where I lived in Oakland, many of the men complained about their probation officers. I saw this as a way of helping my community. My summers were spent in court, listening to cases."

Carpenter knew that college would not be easy, but she did not realize how hard it would be until she tried to combine school, work, and family. By then, her family also included a young son, Vincent. "My family responsibilities did not disappear . . . [I]n the beginning of our marriage, we could not afford a washing machine. I used a washing board and tin tub. I still had to cook and clean and care for my family." Carpenter tried to do it all until one evening when she rushed home from work to prepare dinner before going to school. "I put leftover red beans on the stove. I did not realize that all the beans had been eaten, and all that was left was the juice. I stirred up a batch of corn bread and popped it in the oven and turned the oven too high. I put on a pan of rice and, while the food was cooking, I put my husband's shirts in the recently purchased washing machine. I did not realize that one of his colored T-shirts was among his best shirts. Since he wore white dress shirts to work each day, this was disastrous.

"When my husband came home, he dug into the pot of rice, which had burned and came up with black from the bottom. He reached for the beans and discovered that nothing was left but juice. And the corn bread looked beautiful on the outside, but was mushy on the inside. It was then that we both realized that I could not do it all, and he had to help with the household responsibilities if I were to complete college."

"While I was growing up," says *Essence* magazine's editor-in-chief Susan Taylor, " . . . a college education [wasn't] stressed in my family. Instead, my parents stressed independence, hard work, and entrepreneurship. I don't know if my father was a high school graduate; my mother was not. They did, however, have a tremendous grasp of English grammar. My mother was the force behind my early education. My brother and I went to Catholic school, because my mother felt that we were not getting the proper education in public school. I was born and baptized an Episcopalian—then suddenly we became Catholics . . . Because she wanted a better education for us, she changed her faith to Catholicism. In those days, at least one parent had to be Catholic." Taylor and her brother went to Catholic school until the eighth grade, when they again enrolled in the public school system. By then, the family had moved from Harlem to Queens, where they bought a single-family home in a better neighborhood. To Taylor and her brother, it was like moving to the country.

Anxious to enter the world of work, Taylor took her first job as an office assistant immediately after graduating from high school. Before beginning her career at *Essence,* she also worked as an actress, a modeling instructor, and the owner of her own cosmetics company. It was not until a portion of her responsibilities as editor-in-chief at the magazine required that she host a television show that Taylor felt a need for more intellectual and historical information. "When I was suddenly interviewing heavyweights such as Jesse Jackson, Shirley Chisholm, and James Baldwin, I realized I didn't know enough about the world and the people in it. My confidence began to weaken. When I discussed with my friends my plans to take college courses, many of them discouraged me. They did not think that I needed to go back to school. Many of them who had university degrees thought that I had achieved more than they. But the feeling of not being quite prepared would not go away. I returned to my quiet time, to my spiritual center, and asked myself, 'How is your life? Are you ordering it in a way that is helping you to grow? Are you doing your best work at work? Are you feeling confident? . . . When I acknowledged my own truth, I knew that I had to return to school. In 1985, I enrolled at Fordham University, registered, and selected the courses that interested me.

"When I returned to school, I did not have a degree in mind; I just wanted to know more about people throughout the world. I was particularly interested in the history of African peoples throughout the world. I did not have an understanding of . . . important historical events, and my teachers at school had not taught the history of black people . . . You see, I was not interested in academics when I was in high school. I wanted to be an actress. I just wanted to get out of high school and away from my parents. I wanted to move into my own apartment and get on with my life. And that is what I did. My primary goal has always been to be an independent person.

"After attending Fordham University for a few years, I decided to talk with [an] advisor, who discovered that I had enough social science courses to declare a major. The adviser informed me that I could graduate by following a set curriculum." In May 1991, Taylor received a bachelor of arts degree in social science at Fordham University. Her next educational goal is to enroll in the executive M.B.A. program at Columbia.

EDUCATION AND BLACK ENGLISH

As I listened to the women I interviewed, I noticed how articulate they all were. None of them said "is" where "are" was needed or "I" for "me" in a sentence. They did not say "you was" or "fo'" for "four" or "do'" for "door" or "I seen" for "I saw" or make any of the other grammatical errors that are common in the vernacular of many black Americans. Somewhere down the academic road, these women, consciously or not, had made the decision to speak formal English rather than Black English.

For some educators, the vernacular called Black English has become a subject of increasing concern. They perceive—and rightly so, I believe—a lack of standard American English to be a formidable barrier to advancement within the workplace. For anyone of ambition in America—white, black, or brown—the ability to speak English well is an important requirement for career success and is often the measuring rod people will use—rightly or wrongly—to judge an individual's intelligence.

"The ability to write and speak well is paramount to one's success," publisher Ruth Washington said during our interview. "I am saddened by the waste of human potential that I see and read about. I grieve for my community and how it has deteriorated. I see young black people who come to the *Sentinel* for jobs. We can't hire them because they can't read or write well, and their English is atrocious. We talk about competing in the world economy, but some of us can't compete on the local level. If we think we have it tough today, just think how it will be when we are asked to not only speak English grammatically . . . , but to also learn . . . Spanish and Japanese."

A few years ago, some scholars felt that black people should hold on to their language as long as they could be understood. However, teachers and school officials are beginning to realize the importance of each child's ability to speak standard English correctly.

In *Black Majority,* Peter Woods discusses the challenges that have confronted blacks from the beginning of their lives in America. Although many slaves, such as orator and former slave Frederick Douglass, were able to master the English language, they were careful to hide this facility because of the general attitude among whites that "smart" blacks could be dangerous. Others were not eager to acquire their master's language, believing that speaking the master's tongue was a sign of capitulation. Even today, some black Americans, especially young blacks, are reluctant to speak standard American English, because they believe that it is the white man's language, and Black English belongs to them.

Most American educators have come to believe that the mastery of standard American English is crucial to the future success of every schoolchild in this nation. I am reminded of the mothers and fathers of the women profiled here, who bequeathed their passion for books and learning to their daughters, and how valuable that bequest turned out to be.

THE FUTURE OF EDUCATION IS AMERICA'S FUTURE

A recent study by the American Council on Education revealed a disturbing lack of interest in higher education among black people in this country. Over a twenty-year period, from 1973 to 1993, there was a steady decline in black student enrollment at colleges and universities.

What has happened to account for this trend? Has that holy grail called education lost its value in the eyes of black parents today? Has the fire in the belly—that longing for learning—gone out in an entire generation of youngsters? Do their parents cherish education less than the parents and grandparents who came before them? Have black parents abandoned their responsibility to help their children get the best education possible?

"We cannot stand by and watch our children fail and end up in jail," Vivian Bowser told me, echoing the sentiments of all thirty-two of the women I interviewed for this book. "Success in the twenty-first century depends on the ability of all Americans." Legislators and the citizens who elect them must wake up to the fact that America as a whole will suffer unless all of our children are given the chance they need—as well as the discipline and encouragement—to achieve their greatest potential.

CHAPTER 5

ABOVE RACISM AND SEXISM

"I remember going often to hear the New Orleans Philharmonic Orchestra and sitting in the "buzzard's gallery." One day, after one of the concerts, I went backstage, where they looked at me very, very, strangely. I went up to the first flutist, and said, 'I'd like to study with you.' He looked at me and asked, 'You, a Negro, study with me?' I looked him straight in the eyes and said, 'Yes, Sir.' I think I was thirteen at the time. After the shock wore off, and he heard me play, just like that this fine orchestral flutist became my first classical teacher. My parents took me to his home for lessons until we moved to another city." —D. ANTOINETTE HANDY

BEFORE HER RETIREMENT in 1993, Antoinette Handy's office was located in the Old Post Office building in Washington, D.C., which housed an up-scale shopping mall in addition to the executive offices on its top floors. Handy's suite of offices was a beehive of activity, with documents and books everywhere. When I came to interview her, she greeted me warmly, directing me to one of the few chairs that was empty of documents.

A nationally respected solo and orchestral flutist, musicologist, and arts administrator, Handy was an educator at several colleges and universities before accepting the position of assistant director of music programs at the National Endowment for the Arts (NEA). In 1990, she became the director of music programs.

The NEA, established by Congress in 1965, has fourteen programs. The music program, the largest among them, has an annual budget of more than ten million dollars, with a mandate to provide outreach, encouragement, and financial support for musical excellence in the United States. Symphony orchestras, choruses, chamber and jazz ensembles, solo singers, instrumentalists, and training institutes—most facets of the world of music in this country—have benefited from grants awarded by the NEA.

Handy has experienced both good times and challenging times, but told me that she has never regretted the choices she made, nor her decision to "buck the system" when doing so would make a difference. She is committed to meeting head-on each educational and artistic challenge that faces her and says that she will continue to seek ways to eliminate racial and cultural inequities in the arts. Handy's story is a perfect example of what it takes for a talented, intelligent black woman to beat back the vestiges of racism and sexism and succeed in her chosen profession. She was hell-bent on accomplishing her goals despite the barriers placed in her way.

Born in New Orleans in 1930, Handy is a minister's daughter and the youngest of four children. Her mother, a pianist, began teaching each child to play the piano at the age of five. When they were six, she taught them the violin. "I set out to be a musician at an early age but did not know which instrument to focus on. I liked the sound of a symphony orchestra and felt that was where I belonged; but blacks did not play in symphony orchestras when I was growing up, so I had no African American role models to look up to."

After graduating from high school in New Orleans, Handy enrolled at Spelman College in Atlanta. Spelman, founded in 1881, was the first college created specifically for African American women in the United States. Handy recalled that Spelman's liberal arts program was one of the finest in the country; but the school's music department had limited resources. "Although I received a solid academic education at Spelman, I needed the solid foundation in music education. I was getting a lot of exposure as a flutist, playing at various college-sponsored concerts; but the one thing I needed and was not getting was classical instruction."

Handy eventually convinced her father that she could not compete as a classical flutist without better training. She also told him that she had applied to, and been accepted at, the New England Conservatory of Music in Boston.

"When my father came to take me from Spelman to Boston, Dr. Florence Matilda Read, the last white president of Spelman, asked to meet with us. Dr. Read tried to persuade my father that I owed it to my race to remain at Spelman, where I could make a greater contribution to my community. I felt differently. How could I make a contribution if I did not get the best training possible?"

Coming from the South, racism was a reality for Handy. And yet she was not prepared for the brand of racism she encountered at the New England Conservatory of Music. When Handy entered the conservatory, her counselors made it clear that pursuing an orchestral major would be a waste of her time as well as everyone else's. "The school felt that there were no opportunities for blacks in symphony orchestras. I refused to accept their counsel. I was arrogant enough, even at that time, to think I could help open doors."

Soon after she arrived at the conservatory, Handy was told that she could not live in the women's dormitory. "The school told me that there were no vacancies. Instead, I was offered a room with a black family 'across the tracks.' Because the husband in the family was dying in the back room, I had to share the other bedroom with his wife. When my father saw the situation, and that there was no door to our bedroom, he tried to persuade me to leave. I decided to stay." Several months later, Handy discovered that there were vacant rooms in the dormitories. The hidden policy was to exclude blacks. Two years after she arrived, the school integrated its housing, opening the dorms to students of all races.

Handy recalled other forms of racism she encountered: One of the sororities, Sigma Alpha Iota, invited her to join their organization. She was excited about this apparent honor until a few days later, when the invitation was rescinded. Apparently, the national office had found out that Handy was black. The following year, when restrictions were removed, the sorority again invited her to join. This time Handy refused.

"Although I did not join Sigma Alpha Iota, I did want to become a member of the prestigious national music society, Phi Kappa Lamda. I believed that the organization had not invited me to join because of my race. When I left Boston to work on my graduate degree at Northwestern University in Chicago, the society overlooked me again. Membership in this society is solely based on scholarship, grades, and performance. So at Northwestern, I decided to challenge the oversight. When I asked my advisor about the omission, he told me that I needed a 3.5 average. He hadn't seen my transcript: I had a 4.0 average. He then brought up the question of performance. I told him that I had participated in many excellent, highly regarded recitals and concerts during the year, and the symphony president had told me that my graduate recital was one of the finest of the year. The next day I received my invitation by registered mail."

During her studies at Northwestern, Handy performed with the Civic Orchestra affiliated with the Chicago Symphony—the oldest and one of the best-established training orchestras in the nation. However, following graduation, there were no offers for a permanent position. "I had mixed emotions when I received my cherished master's in fine arts degree in 1953, and the bachelor of music degree [. . .] in 1952; they represented important credentials into the world of music. But I had to face a disappointing reality—there was no place for me in symphony orchestras in America." She had to make the painful decision to redirect her career, choosing one of the few options available to blacks with graduate degrees in music at that time—teaching at a black college.

At the college Handy chose in Florida, she clashed with a deeply entrenched status-quo system that was not quite as insidious as the racism she had experienced throughout her earlier life, but just as frustrating. Any new and creative ideas on the part of faculty were greeted with suspicion, and one had to accept the system or leave. After one semester of academic frustration, she left. "I arrived at the college full of a sense of purpose. I thought I could make a difference, and the students responded to my enthusiasm—the college did not."

While still in her teaching position, Handy wrote a challenging letter to the New Orleans Philharmonic Orchestra that won her an audition.

They didn't offer her a job, but they did extend an invitation to solo with the orchestra, which she accepted.

After leaving Florida, Handy returned to Chicago for a few months, and then left for Europe for a year, where there were many opportunities for her to play in symphony orchestras. Upon returning to America, Handy met and married her husband, Dr. Calvin Montgomery Miller, and joined the faculty at Tuskegee, where her father had gone to school. Later, she and her husband taught at Jackson State University, and then at Virginia State, before she accepted the job as assistant director of music at the National Endowment for the Arts, eventually becoming director of the program.

"In certain areas of classical music," says Handy, "it is still difficult to break the barrier, especially in conducting. There was a young African American woman who had excellent classical training, and all of the attributes and credentials necessary to become a conductor, but she did not get the breaks. I told her that she was not the 'in thing' right now. Fortunately, she did not sit around and wait for the breaks in this country. She conducts in Europe, where there are opportunities for women to work. One problem is that she is getting older, and most of the programs to assist conductors [are directed] toward younger people."

POWER AND PRIVILEGE

As I got older and left the protection of my mother's bosom, I began to question and take notice of events around me. I came to understand the shame and disgrace of discrimination. I began to understand why my mother had us go to the bathroom before leaving home. I understood why she took us to the black neighborhood movie theater instead of the Majestic Theater or other downtown movies where we would have to sit upstairs in the "Crows' Nest," a tiny area reserved for blacks.

Racism comes in many forms. Although as an adult I have never experienced overt racism, throughout my life I have experienced covert racism. I know that I have been denied opportunities because of my difference. As a young adult, I was made aware of an unspoken tradition of many upscale restaurants to seat black couples in less appealing locations near the bathroom, the kitchen, and the serving area. Being aware of this policy, I have refused to be seated in those areas.

We also have in this country widespread ignorance bred from centuries of racist thinking. When my father died a few years ago, I naturally wanted to take some days off from work. I told my boss that I wanted to help my stepmother, my sister, and my daughter arrange for my father's burial. I did not by any stretch of the imagination go with hat in hand; and yet my boss proceeded to tell me, with the utmost kindness and discretion, that the staff would take up a collection for my father's funeral. I smiled, thanked him, and told him that would not be necessary. Granted, most minorities where I worked had low-paying maintenance jobs; I was the only black person in management. But by what logic, apart from racist assumptions, did my boss come to think that I was asking for a handout? It suddenly dawned on me that my boss did not know me, nor I him. I did not know who his parents were or what they did; and he evidently did not know that my father had worked for the federal government for more than forty years and that my stepmother was a school administrator.

Not long after this incident, a neighbor of my parents—who was also a board member of a major organization attending a conference at the convention center where I worked—got into conversation with my boss. He learned from her that she and my parents were two of the first black families to live in our formerly all-white El Cerrito, California, neighborhood. Our families had bought two of the five custom-built homes on a hill that overlooks the Pacific Ocean from the back and a private golf course from the front. I did not blame my boss for falling prey to one of hundreds of stereotypes regarding minorities. But I doubt that he'll ever make that particular mistake again.

REFUSING TO TAKE NO FOR AN ANSWER

During Jewel Plummer Cobb's childhood, her family had little interaction with whites. "As a child I knew that I lived in a black world. So my awareness of racism was through those experiences. I was aware that those people were white over there, and we were black over here. I knew that my physician father could not play golf on public or private courses in Chicago. If he wanted to play, he had to drive twenty-five miles away, to Gary, Indiana."

Cobb was also aware that blacks could ride the buses and sit anywhere in the movie theaters in Chicago, but they could not go into the restaurants downtown. "We, of course, had our own cafes in our neighborhood. Most of our activities revolved around a small demographic area. We were members of a church in the community, and I was a member of both the YMCA and the YWCA for Negroes. I learned to swim at the YMCA. There was also the Regal Theater, where big bands performed. Cab Calloway and Count Basie and other big-time artists played there. Things were quite confusing, but blacks had no problem remembering 'their place' in the gigantic scheme of things."

Donzaleigh Abernathy remembers one night when her childhood innocence may have put her father in danger. "Daddy used to tell the story about driving to the country to see Grandmother. My sister and I would always stay up and talk to him, no matter how many miles we were going or how late. We wanted him to have company. We had a station wagon, and my mother and my brother would fall asleep in the back. One night as we drove down Highway 80, we asked Daddy for hamburgers. Highway 80, which ran between Selma and Montgomery, Alabama, was a dangerous highway, where many people had lost their lives during the civil rights movement. The famous Selma-Montgomery March was down this highway. It was also where Detroit civil rights activist Viola Liuzzo was shot and killed.

"We were on him so badly that, wanting to please us, my father pulled over to this run-down truck-stop and gathered all his nerve. He thought, 'I'm going to feed my children, but I might lose my life in the process.' It showed the kind of courage he had. When he entered the front door, all the people in the cafe stared at him, and he was told that he could not be served in the front but had to go to the side to get the hamburgers. While waiting at the kitchen door, he thought that they might decide to kill him. You see, he had already been beaten unmercifully by Al Lingo and left on the side of the road for dead. Al Lingo, at that time, was director of safety for the city of Birmingham. The way my father always told the story was humorous, but the situation was extremely dangerous. He conquered his fears to feed his children. He was a tremendous father."

The school system in Washington, D.C., was segregated when Eloise Greenfield was growing up there. "Most of the books were hand-me-downs that had been previously used by the students at the white school. Many of the public facilities in the nation's capital were segregated, including the restaurants, soda fountains, theaters, and swimming pools... One federal office where I worked briefly was run like a plantation: There were white people who would not speak [to blacks]."

Susan Taylor recalls, "The nuns in Catholic school let us black students know that we were different. The black girls never got to play the Blessed Mother during Christmas. We were never the special angels. In class we were never favorite students. I remember my first personal racial experience during that time. I had a good friend, Antoinette Bruno, who would often come to my house. She was Italian. One day she wanted me to walk home with her. When we reached her house, she stopped me at the stoop. She told me that I could not go in, that I had to wait on the outside until she returned. She explained that her father would be upset if he found out that she had a black friend. I felt hurt and embarrassed for her."

For some women, signs of discrimination and prejudice were felt in indirect ways. Philanthropist and art collector Eileen Norton was confused and puzzled when her white friends began leaving her school. "I grew up in Watts during the '60s, but my mother usually sent me to the next school over. My junior high school, Henry Clay, was in a neighborhood of tract homes that was in transition. We owned our home, but housing projects were all around us. This was in the '60s, and black families were beginning to move into the tract homes, and their children were beginning to attend Henry Clay. The white kids I started with in the seventh grade were not there in the ninth grade. It was a total change from white to black. It seemed like every week white kids were saying,

'Oh, I'm moving to Orange County. Or, I'm moving to the Valley.' It was unbelievable. I would share with my mother, 'So-and-so is moving.' She tried to explain to me what was happening. I realize now that it was a blatant demonstration of 'white flight.'

"Later, when I entered high school at Hamilton High, I became aware of another kind of racism. The counselors refused to put me in the classes needed in order to go to UCLA, the university I had always wanted to attend. My teachers assumed that since you were black and came from certain schools, you were unprepared, mentally or academically, to go to college. The counselors finally agreed to give me college prep classes, but for the California State colleges. The state colleges had lower academic requirements than UCLA or the other UC campuses. The counselors would tell me that the classes were the same. And I would ask them, 'If the classes were the same, why do you have a Cal State track and a UCLA track?' The more they told me that, the harder I fought until I finally got the program I needed to go to UCLA. It was a real battle. I was not in the South; I was in Los Angeles, not too long ago."

It was not until Betye Saar graduated from high school and entered Pasadena College as an art student that she first experienced the effects of racism. "Our class was chosen as one of the classes to design floats for the New Year's Rose Parade, an annual event known throughout the world. I did not expect to win first, second, or third prize for my design and was extremely happy to win an honorable mention. But before it was presented to me, the award was rescinded. I was just out of high school and had no experience in competing, so to have received even an honorable mention was important to me. When the committee found out that I was black, they gave me tickets to the Rose Bowl game and a cash award instead of my honorable mention. I had complicated their whole selection process." Saar believes that her scholastic abilities and artistic talent helped her overcome other prejudices she might have encountered. "When I entered UCLA as a design major, I felt immediate acceptance. I was a serious student and had the advantage of working with other students who also took their studies seriously."

When Cynthia Shepard Perry was in junior high, the city of Terre

Haute, Indiana, integrated its schools. Since Terre Haute had a very small percentage of black Americans, Perry was one of a few black students in a sea of white faces. "It never occurred to me that whites thought that they were better than we were. In high school I was at the top of my class academically and very active scholastically. The white kids were very solicitous of me.

"It was not until my senior year that I found out what the white students really thought about the black students, including me." Perry had been the only black student in her class since junior high school. When she reached tenth grade, another black girl was assigned to her class. "One day, one of the white girls who had been a very close friend whispered to me, 'Cynthia, we like you very much, but we don't like that other nigger.' I was shocked! My white friend had let me know where I stood in the scheme of things. That experience taught me an important lesson: I became determined to succeed in spite of what others thought or did to control my life. In fact, I was voted by my class the most likely to succeed."

At one point in her career, Terri Wright accepted a position as administrative officer for AIDS issues within the Connecticut State Department of Health. "They did not know what to do with a highly educated, professional black woman. If you were a secretary or a janitor or an office manager [. . .], okay. But if you were someone who asked hard questions, challenged the system [. . .], they were very threatened."

Jackie Tatum has felt the negative effects of bias more in Los Angeles as an adult than she had in Kansas City during her childhood. "My eyes were wide open to it, but I realized that it was quite subtle in California. It was there; you felt it. My grandmother explained to me when I was quite young that there would be problems that we must face in one way or another. She said that when we came to California from Kansas I would experience 'separate but equal' on a different level. In California it would be more covert, less overt. My grandmother was right."

Tatum gives an example of trying to buy a house during the 1960s in the up-scale Baldwin Hills section of Los Angeles. She and her husband had to look at the house they wanted after dark, so the white homeowners wouldn't know that a black couple was planning to buy in their neighborhood. "The realtors would not openly sell homes to blacks in Baldwin Hills."

Publisher Ruth Washington cautioned that racism must not be blamed for every negative thing that happens to black people. "We have corrupt black leaders just like we have corrupt white leaders. We have racist black people, just as we have racist white people. We have people [who], when they get caught with their hands in the cookie jar, yell racism.

"Mr. Washington, my husband, was a leader in many crusades against discrimination in the workplace and where black people shopped. In the '40s, he and other prominent black leaders led boycotts against the Central Avenue white businesses, who got rich off the profits of the black consumers, but refused to hire them to work in the stores. But every time a black person is denied an opportunity for a job or every time something negative happens to us, we can't always attribute it to racism. Many times we are not qualified for the job. Competition is keen in the job market. We have to make sure that we can compete. We don't want people to give us anything. We must have the education, the training, and the experience.

"When we first started in this business, the *Sentinel* was able to get the best and the brightest black journalists and newspaper staff, because white papers weren't hiring them. Like everything else, as soon as equal opportunities in hiring became law, our people preferred working for white newspapers. We continue to hire the best and the brightest, but it gets harder and harder to find good workers. We turn down more applicants than we hire, because people are just not qualified—but not because they are black or white."

SEXISM AND THE BLACK WOMAN

The psychological toll that racism and sexism have taken on black women can be measured by the historical accumulation of injustices that society has condoned. To beat the system, black women have had to learn to understand the white male system from the inside out. "We have to operate within both worlds if we are to succeed," says investment banker Iris Rideau. "I learned that years ago. Remember, I am competing with the big guns, such as Paine Webber, Crowell Weedon, and Merrill Lynch. They are thinking while most of us are sleeping. It's important that I stay in step with them."

In the late 1940s, when Norma Sklarek applied to Columbia University's school of architecture, there was a strict quota system for women. Sklarek was admitted on the strength of her scientific background and an outstanding scholastic record. "Other colleges at Columbia may have had similar gender and racial quotas, but it was quite obvious in architecture. The school didn't want to waste space on women. They felt that women would get married and return home to have children.

"The competition was fierce. I entered with a minimum requirement of one year of liberal arts, whereas many of my male classmates had bachelor's or master's degrees. Some of the students were World War II veterans receiving financial aid from the G.I. Bill. Other students had work experience as draftsmen. I was the youngest in class, competing with mature, experienced men.

"After graduation I took the licensing exam—thirty-six hours over four days—and passed it the first time. This surprised many people. When I went back to visit the dean of the school, he told me that not even some straight-A students in the class had passed the entire exam the first time."

Sexism and the old-boy network are just part of the challenge women have to fight and overcome, according to NASA researcher Pat Cowings. "Any woman, particularly a professional woman, has experienced chauvinism and sexism. I think experiencing them both at once is the hardest of all. An example of sexism occurred just after I received my doctorate, [when I] was a researcher at Rockefeller University. One morning, Dr. Neil Miller, a highly respected researcher, scheduled a meeting in his office with his principal investigators. At the meeting were the chief of cardiology from Cornell and the chief of neurology from Albert Einstein Hospital. As the meeting was about to begin, one of the investigators leaned over and asked me if I would get him a cup of coffee. I pointed toward the direction of the coffee pot. He then asked, 'Aren't you taking notes?' Bless Dr. Miller, who was leading the program. 'No, no,' he said, 'Dr. Cowings is one of my principal investigators. Please feel free to get your own coffee.'"

When she'd finished this story, Cowings handed me a coffee mug that had been sitting on her desk. "Someone gave me this coffee cup recently." On the outside of the mug was written, "Whatever a woman does, she must do it twice as well as a man to be considered half as good." In large letters inside the cup I read, "Fortunately this is not difficult." "Women really do have to perform better than average to be considered average," said Cowings as I handed the mug back to her. "A woman has to acquire an attitude of pigheadedness in order to prevail."

Brenda Bass is a Beverly Hills pediatrician. When she entered medical school, she was originally attracted to the challenges and potential rewards of surgery. She also knew that prevailing attitudes in the medical establishment would have made this an almost impossible field for her, not only as a woman, but as a black woman. "I guess the biggest difficulty was the fact that black female medical students in white majority universities were double minorities . . . I went to an all-black undergraduate school, Fisk University in Nashville, Tennessee, where there was academic and social support. During my medical school years and during my residency in Los Angeles, the majority of the students, the instructors, and the doctors were white. There was no support system to help make life easier. So often it is said of a black person in a field dominated by whites that black people have to be better in order to gain the same respect. It is true in my field, and that is a very formidable obstacle to try and overcome.

"If you try something, and it doesn't work out the first time—if you throw your hands up and walk away, it can never be accomplished. Intelligence probably has less to do with [overcoming barriers] than persistence and the ability to be comfortable with who you are. I know a lot of people who have great business sense who don't have a formal education, and they have had great success."

I asked Dr. Bass which of the two, racism or sexism, had created the greatest challenges for her as a doctor. "As a student it was both; but as a licensed physician, I think my age and sex are more of a negative than the color of my skin. Some people think I'm attractive. This is an additional negative. It's a double-edged sword. If I say something I consider important, it is not taken as seriously as it would be from a white male or white female."

PBS executive Jennifer Lawson does not feel that she has ever been passed over for a promotion or that her career was ever jeopardized by the old-boy network. Art scholar Mary Jane Hewitt feels convinced that the old-boy network is part of the challenge that every woman has to fight and overcome. "I first became aware of sexism when I enrolled at the University of Minnesota. I did not, at first, recognize it as sexism, because at the elementary and secondary level, most of my teachers were women. It was a sudden shift from many female teachers to just a few. When I finally got a woman professor, I was eager to know more about her. How did she break into this closed club [of] college faculty professors? She was outstanding, she was young, and she was brilliant. I thought it was wonderful to know this wonderful woman. There were no blacks on the faculty at that time."

The academic community, according to Hewitt, continues to be one of the most closed old-boy clubs around. "It's everywhere. It's national. This seat of enlightenment called the university is the most sexist, bigoted of institutions. Yes, I've run into this club, but I've never let it defeat me. I know it's there, but I have this thing that my mother pounded into me when I was young: 'Don't make your plans based on what is, but on what it might be.' So I go on doing what I want to do and getting where I want to go, in spite of the barriers that are placed in front of me."

In the early '40s, when Rev. Ella P. Mitchell tried to get into Yale University's School of Theology, her application was rejected because they had no fieldwork opportunities for women, especially for black women. After she received her doctorate in 1974 at the Claremont School of Theology in California and decided that it was time to preach, institutional sexism again stood in her path and blocked her way. "For many years, I thought that teaching would be my ministry; I was not sure I wanted to preach. When I decided to make application for ordination, I thought that I would be easily accepted." It was not until a full year after she made application that a minister finally took Mitchell's request seriously. After they talked, he assembled an ordination council and set the date and time for the ceremonies. Plans were made in early summer, but by August the minister decided that he could not follow through with Mitchell's ordination. Significantly, he called Mitchell's husband, who is also a minister, rather than break the news to her directly. "I was quite disheartened by this minister's refusal to ordain me. He told my husband that the Holy Spirit had led him to say no. I will not question his reason, but black female ministers are not welcome in many churches. Only a few are open to receive us. That may be the reason [why] there are so few ordained Baptist women ministers." A short time later, a family friend and colleague, Reverend J. Alfred Smith, called and agreed to ordain her. "Reverend Smith was aware of my religious experience and respected my credentials."

Mitchell believes that until the Baptist congregations, for the most part composed of women, and the ministers, who are almost all men, understand that another kind of voice is needed in the church, black women ministers will continue to be left out of mainstream ministries.

Bishop Leontine Kelly, the first African American female elected bishop of the United Methodist Church, agrees that sexism is entrenched throughout the religious community. Kelly explained that female ministers, especially in the South, have had to vigorously confront a tightly knit sexist network. "It's called the 'blessed old-boy network,' in our parlance," she said. "Women are still not accepted as ministers or as equals by some male ministers and, in part, by some congregations. It is like, 'How dare you aspire to the Episcopates.' It is not the problem of qualification or credentials, it is just not an area that 'women should be in.' Change is very hard for some male ministers to accept. It is as if you are being unfaithful and disloyal to the church."

Before the conference at which Kelly was nominated to the bishopric, one of the black ministers called to ask for her support at the general conference. She told him that she would vote for him if he voted for her. He then asked, 'Why? You are not going to run!' I said, 'Of course, I am.'" Kelly feels that this "virus" is implanted in the male system. "Some men believe that it is their birthright to have the power and the control and the decision-making privileges. When women attempt to change the rules, the barriers are thrown up. Those of us who are black and female have to cope with the white male power structure, which is both racist and sexist, and chauvinistic black male ministers. There is also the game of playing the black woman against the black male. We want to support our males; but, at the same time, we can't relinquish all that has been gained basically through our own efforts."

Kelly insists that black women have to demand respect from both white and black men. Once she was elected bishop, men—especially the black ministers—were extremely cooperative. "There is a way of working with those who have a different point of view than yours," she noted with a diplomacy worthy of her high office.

CHAPTER 6

CIVIL RIGHTS AND THE WOMEN'S MOVEMENT

"We moved to Atlanta in the early '60s. Uncle Martin wanted Daddy in Atlanta, because the new headquarters for the civil rights movement was Atlanta. Daddy didn't want to leave his church, First Baptist, and his loyal membership, who stood with him when the church was severely damaged by a bomb during the Montgomery Bus Boycott. Mother did not want to leave Montgomery either. But Uncle Martin encouraged Daddy to relocate and found him a church. —DONZALEIGH ABERNATHY

D
ONZALEIGH ABERNATHY is a child of the civil rights movement. The daughter of famed civil rights leader, Reverend Ralph David Abernathy, Donzaleigh was born in Montgomery, Alabama, home of the historic Montgomery Bus Boycott, where the Movement won its first victory. "I can remember separate water fountains," says Abernathy. "I remember needing to go to the restroom in public places, but not being allowed to . . . [W]hen they did have toilets for 'coloreds,' you didn't want to use them, because they were filthy."

In 1994 I met Donzaleigh Abernathy at a Martin Luther King birthday celebration. She told me about the atmosphere of her household after her father had been convinced by "Uncle Martin" to relocate from Montgomery to Atlanta in 1961. "[M]any of the staff meetings were held at our house. My mother was a tremendous cook, which she doesn't like to admit to—but I think that is the reason they chose to meet at our house. A lot of knowledgeable adults were in and out of our home, and they spoke on a level that I, as a child, was captivated with, appreciated, and wanted so much to be a part of . . . [This was the period] when I developed this quest for knowledge and became an avid reader. There were people from all walks of life that came to be a part of history. We had white ministers that came to live with us, such as Bud Walker and Glenn Smiley, the man who taught Daddy and Uncle Martin the principles of nonviolence during the Montgomery Bus Boycott. Gertrude Angling came to live with us from Sweden, just to participate in this great movement. Mahalia Jackson, the famous gospel singer, and Harry Belafonte visited. As a little girl I was privileged to meet many great men and women who worked in the Movement; but I took them all for granted, since they were always in my life.

"My father and I were very close. He had studied acting like I did when he was in college. I wanted to be an artist, and he wanted me to be whatever I wanted to be. He used to say, 'Dream, Donzaleigh, and make those dreams a reality.' . . . When he wrote his book, *The Walls Came Tumbling Down*, he gave me the first chapter—which he loved the most—to read and make notes, because he respected my writing ability and my opinion. As far as being an actress, without a doubt he encouraged that more than anything. My mother would have much preferred that I had gotten an M.B.A. and become a businesswoman or a lawyer. But I am an artist, a creative person. The business side of my brain does not function the way the creative side does . . .

"I remember seeing Marlon Brando and Sidney Poitier at the March on Washington. I wanted to do what they did. Politicians were a given in my life, therefore I did not aspire to anything political. You always want that which is different.

"We kids were taken on all of the major marches. Daddy was insistent about that. We went to the March on Washington, the Selma-Montgomery March, to Chicago, Memphis, and many others. I've been tear-gassed. I remember when I was at the March on Washington, Benjamin E. Mayes, the president of Morehouse College, grabbed me and kept me from falling down. He cautioned me to be careful where I ran. He did not want me to hurt myself or fall down the Lincoln

Memorial stairs. He was very nice and grandfatherly. At that time, I had no idea that the Benjamin Mayes I knew was a great educator and philosopher. Like all the other famous and respected people in the Movement, he was a familiar face in my life . . .

"People didn't know Uncle Martin and my daddy; they know the legend of Martin Luther King, Jr., and Ralph David Abernathy. They don't know the father, the husband, the person, the human being. I knew the persons, and I feel obliged to tell the beautiful stories of those beautiful men that I lived with and loved—the stories of my father and his best friend, Martin Luther King, Jr. It's a debt of love that I owe them. Uncle Martin said in a speech that he delivered in Birmingham at the 16th Street Baptist Church, 'There are some who make history, there are some who experience history, and there are some who write history. I don't know how many historians we have here tonight at 16th Street, but we today are making history.' I was not there when he spoke those words, but I was there during that time in history. I experienced it, I witnessed it, and I have to tell it."

WE SHALL OVERCOME

For PBS executive Jennifer Lawson, the early '60s were a time when student involvement helped correct more than 400 years of indignities, mistreatment, and laws limiting the opportunities and narrowing the destinies of black people. "As soon as I arrived at Tuskegee Institute, I saw civil rights activities all around me. The fact that black people could make a difference in their lives energized me. My conscience told me that I had to be part of it." There was an excitement in the air that Lawson, a young pre-med student from Birmingham, Alabama, could not ignore. In the town of Tuskegee and the surrounding rural areas, social activism was stirring up the black population. Human rights and the right to vote dominated the minds and prayers of every black person in the area.

Lawson decided to seize the moment, convinced that she could make a meaningful contribution toward helping to eradicate segregation in the South, and gain civil and social rights—including the right to vote—for

black people. Like Donzaleigh Abernathy, she saw her chance to participate in making history.

Torn between her commitment to the civil rights movement and
commitment to school, Lawson finally decided that she couldn't do both;
she left Tuskegee in her first year to work full-time for the Student
Nonviolent Coordinating Committee (SNCC). "I lived on almost nothing, slept out of a sleeping bag, and ate lots of crackers. Many of the
Tuskegee teachers, black and white, supported our efforts and sent
money to help us.

"The time was ripe for leaders such as Martin Luther King of the
Southern Christian Leadership Conference and Stokely Carmichael of
SNCC to break the back of Jim Crow laws that controlled the human and
civil rights of black people. One of SNCC's tactics was to hold demon-
strations at lunch counters and other facilities that refused to serve
blacks. We also registered people to vote. Many of the students went to
jail and refused to pay fines or bail, choosing instead to serve their sen-
tences. This was an extremely important time, and one for which I would
risk my life. I knew it was dangerous. I personally knew a classmate who
was killed during that time. There were several people . . . [who died] for
the cause."

Lawson left SNCC in 1967. "I was very much a believer in the civil
rights movement, but it began to change. Urban movements like the
Black Panthers were developing under the leadership of Huey Newton
and Eldridge Cleaver. I was not convinced that these new approaches
were valid. The whole notion of people marching with guns was a different world from what I had envisioned for the future. I wasn't sure that
I wanted to be a part of this new movement."

Lawson went on to work for the National Council of Negro Women
as a field representative, working side by side with Fannie Lou Hamer,
who founded the Mississippi Freedom Democratic Party. In the Council,
Lawson worked on community development projects such as low-
income housing for some of the poorest people in the country.
Eventually she left the Council and worked for two years in Tanzania,
East Africa, where she found a similarly high degree of illiteracy. It was

in Tanzania that Lawson came full circle, becoming convinced that education was the answer to many of the ills of the poor. She packed her bags, boarded a plane, and returned to the United States to work toward her dream of making education universally accessible through the communications media.

Marriage and the birth of her daughters prevented artist Betye Saar from going South to be with others who were putting their lives on the line. "Although I was not down there getting beaten up, jailed, and killed, I was deeply affected by the civil rights movement, and knew that I had to make a statement. People were trying to exercise their rights to an equal existence, and they were being bitten by dogs and hosed with high-powered commercial fire hoses, and all that other demeaning stuff. I knew I had to protest in some way, so I did it through my art. One thing I did was take derogatory images like Uncle Tom and Aunt Jemima and Little Black Sambo—things that perpetuated racism and submissiveness—and recycled them into militant figures. They made powerful statements.

"A lot of my work during the '60s evolved from my anger over what was happening in the South and the death of Dr. Martin Luther King, Jr. That was the turning point and my personal reality in facing up to the fact of racism. Actually, here we are in the '90s, and we are still struggling with that issue."

Mary Jane Hewitt, an internationally recognized expert and editor in the field of African American art, was working as an interpreter-translator for the U.S. government in Paris when the civil rights movement was in full bloom. "Had it not been for Rosa Parks, I would not be back in this country," Hewitt told me. "I was living in Paris when she sat down and refused to move. I knew that I had to come home. The next year found me in Los Angeles getting active in social issues. I know that many doors have opened for me and other black people because of the Rosa Parkses, the Martin Luther Kings, the Fannie Lou Hamers of this world, the Watts riots, and all the rest."

Kaycee Hale was in Los Angeles during the summer of 1965, when the Watts riots began—in fact, she was standing just a few feet away from where the riots started. "I will never forget the date—August 11, 1965, about seven o'clock in the evening. I lived in Watts at the time and was standing on the corner of Avalon and 116th Street when the police stopped this young man, Marquette Frye, for a traffic violation. What appeared to be a simple, everyday occurrence of a driver getting a traffic ticket turned into one of the most awful moments of my life. Homes and buildings were burned, and businesses were broken into and looted. It was a frightening experience that I hoped would never happen again. I find it sad that twenty-five years later, in 1992, a similar disturbance happened in South Los Angeles. I feel the same as Rodney King when he asked, 'Why can't we get along?'"

BLACK WOMEN AND THE WOMEN'S MOVEMENT

In 1850, antislavery activist Sojourner Truth asked her white audience at a women's suffrage meeting, "Sisters, I aren't clear what ye'd be after. If women want any rights more than they got, why don't they just take 'em and not be talking about it?" [See bibliography—Pauli, H. *Her Name Was Sojourner Truth.*]

Many black women have been reluctant to embrace the women's movement, believing that the National Organization for Women and similar organizations were formed for and by privileged white women. Black women have had to go it alone for so long that forming an alliance with predominantly white organizations has been problematic. As one woman I spoke to put it, "Anything we've gotten, we've gotten on our own." Margaret Wright wrote in *Black Women in White America*, "We don't think work liberates you. We've been doing it so damned long."

Despite the ambivalence of many black women toward the women's movement in this country, many of them have benefited from the opportunities created by white women waging their battles. When I was growing up, women aspired to a handful of professions, mostly in teaching or nursing. A few of my friends who felt that college was a waste of time were able to get jobs as elevator operators or clerical workers. A few others aspired to be airline flight attendants. Barbara Theard was just out of high school when she considered becoming an airline hostess. "It did not take me long to realize, at that time in the '50s, that there were no black flight attendants. So my dream went out the window. Another of my interests was to become a school teacher, which was derailed when I got married and postponed college. I thought that I'd marry and become a housewife and mother. College could come later."

Theard and her husband moved from her birthplace, New Orleans, to Los Angeles, where she thought she would continue her education. "College was accessible and within the financial reach of everyone. My husband had other ideas. He wanted me to work." Theard recalled how her career began. "One day we ran into a friend from home [New Orleans] in our neighborhood market. The friend, who worked at a bank, mentioned that there was a job opening for a switchboard opera-tor and asked if I were interested. I was not interested, but my husband was interested for me. He literally pushed me out the door."

It was not long after Theard started to work at the bank that troubles began at home. Since they were not able to solve their differences, she and her husband separated and later divorced. Theard realized that she would need a better salary if she was going to raise their child on her own. "I took classes and seminars that were offered by the bank in asso-ciation with the American Institute of Banking. At that time, in the '60s, the Bank of America began an aggressive program to bring parity into the workplace by training more women to work in formerly male-spe-cific jobs. It was not easy for me to leave work and go to classes in the evening, because I had a daughter to raise by myself; but I could not ignore the opportunities for advancement. Fortunately, I had a neighbor who looked after my child when she was young. I also used babysitters until she got older. Then she became a latch-key kid."

At Bank of America, Theard advanced through the ranks from switchboard operator, to proofreader, to new accounts manager, to one of the few female black bank tellers at that time. She then went to work in the utilities department, and then into operations. She was an opera-tions officer and, for three years, taught at teller school. "I was a loan officer on a lending program at several branches. I have also been on the accrediting examinations team, which examined loan portfolios at different branches. Needless to say, I have done just about every activity in a bank—and many of the opportunities came about because of the women's movement."

During the '50s, most blacks were assigned to banks in all-black neighborhoods; Theard's bank was no exception. "When I first started, blacks were assigned to the bank on Central Avenue on the East Side, [catering] to an all-black clientele. I worked there for ten years before I was transferred to a more ideal location, a branch on the West side of town."

The opportunities enjoyed in the '60s and '70s by Theard and other people beginning their careers without college degrees are no longer available. "Many of the black women I know in banking came into the business around the time I did," Theard explained. "The system and selection procedures have changed from when we got our start. Workers don't come up through the ranks the way we did. When I first started, management encouraged us to take training in order to advance. The classes were free and presented . . . an opportunity to obtain excellent credentials. Now most new managers are college graduates with master's degrees in business administration. I don't see too many young black women coming into banking as managers. Most of the women who are being trained for management are young white . . . M.B.As. Now you must have degrees behind your name if you want to [be promoted] on the professional level."

FEAR OF SUCCESS, FEAR OF FAILURE

Many white women brought up with traditional values have expressed ambiguous feelings about their success in the professional world. Commenting on this, publisher Ruth Washington told me, "There is no question that black women seek and need success in their lives. Theirs is a fear of failure, not a fear of success."

Black women have not historically been placed on pedestals in the way in which white women of a certain type and age have been celebrated and desired in America (I am hard pressed to think of a black equivalent, for instance, to Marilyn Monroe). I've heard some black women say that they would like to experience what white women are rejecting. "I have always worked," Zelma Stennis told me. "At thirteen, I had a part-time job at an appliance store. I believe most black women will tell you the same thing. My focus has been to succeed in everything I do. The fear of failing has kept me on track."

Mary Jane Hewitt agrees. "Every time I try something new, I'm afraid that I might fail. Every time I write an article, I'm afraid that it might be a dud. Every time I make a speech, I'm afraid I'm going to fall flat on my *tuchis*. I'm always afraid of failure, but I do not let it stop me. It motivates me to be as good as possible in everything I do. However, I've never been afraid to walk away from a no-win situation, whether it's a marriage or career or anything. [It's] like the gambler's creed: 'Know when to hold them, and know when to fold them, and know when to walk away.'"

Brenda Bass, M.D., did not fear success, but she remembers a time when she did have second thoughts about divulging her professional prospects to a man she had just met. "I was home for the Christmas holidays and went to a club with friends. This fellow and I were talking, and when we started going through the 'What do you do?' routine, I hesitated. I didn't want to tell him that I was in medical school. . . . As far as achieving my goal to become a physician, I distinctly remember thinking about the impact that my achievment would have on my life. Sometimes it was a little painful to realize that a man will look at you and say, 'You make more than I do'; or 'I'm not willing to fit your hours into my schedule' . . . It was not entirely a fear of success, because mine was not immobilizing: My main goal was to achieve, to be successful . . . [T]he pain was not so bad that it kept me from achieving my goal. But I want to acknowledge the fact that it was there."

WORKING THE NETWORK

Networking is a recent phenomenon for black female professionals simply by virtue of the fact that there have been so few female black professionals in any given field before now, with the possible exception of schoolteachers. The National Coalition of 100 Black Women, founded in the 1980s, was one of the first black women's organizations that made professional networking possible for its membership.

Marketing consultant Dolores Ratcliff believes that most black women do not yet know how to network effectively. "Research tells us that we are three to ten telephone calls away from reaching almost anyone in the world. That is why networking with as many people as possible is important for ongoing contacts; and that is why I wrote my book, *Women Entrepreneurs, Networking, and Sweet Potato Pie: A Business Survival Guide.*" Ratcliffe's book explains the importance of acquiring networking skills, and identifying and resolving networking challenges. She feels that her philosophy on the value of networking is the key to getting around the "old white boy network." "[The title of] my book is a metaphor for surviving [in the business world]. A sweet potato pie appears easy to make, but it isn't. Just as in making a successful pie, there is a series of developmental steps that one has to consciously take [in becoming a successful entrepreneur]."

Friendships, as Terri Wright found out, are a natural and important form of networking for women. "Those friendships that I developed while I was at the University of Michigan proved crucial at one point in my career. I had developed a number of models for infant mortality reduction in the Detroit area and was called to speak throughout the country. I also discovered that my husband had a serious drug problem. We tried hard to work through the problem, without success. After spending months in therapy and counseling, it became clear that we were going nowhere fast—his problem could not be resolved. Also, I was not willing to sacrifice our child and all I had gained and worked hard for.

"He was in another world by then. I lost a great deal of weight because of the stress of home and career. I felt I had a child that needed me, and a job that I loved and did not want to lose, so I got divorced. Fortunately I had two friends from school who had also remained in Detroit. They helped me a lot. I had other mothers with children my son's age, and we swapped the care of the kids on the weekends. Between them and my former husband's family, my child was cared for."

Aleta Carpenter recalls the support she received from several black women station managers when she was president and general manager of a radio station in Oakland, California. "When I was feeling the pressures of work, I would call and talk to one of the women who let me talk while she listened. That is all you need sometimes, someone to listen."

NOBEL Women, the National Organization of Black Elected Legislative Women, was established in 1985 in Philadelphia to meet the unique needs of its membership. State Senator Diane Watson was one of NOBEL's founders: "The female legislators felt they were not taken seriously by male members of their affiliate organization, the National Black Caucus of State Legislators. We were unhappy with the condescending manner in which we were treated and frustrated that our bids for higher offices were not taken seriously."

Despite the gains of the women's movement, there is still a tendency for women to network by race rather than gender. Black women have tended to feel that their interests will not necessarily be served in organizations dominated by white women. There are exceptions, though. Both Vivian Bowser, past president of the Texas Teachers' Association, and Leontine Kelly, a bishop in the United Methodist Church, relied on the strategic planning and teamwork of women from many races and backgrounds to achieve their goals. "Before integration," says Bowser, "there were two separate Texas teachers' assocations fighting for power— one black, one white. Each was geared toward achieving as much clout as possible. The black organization was continually fighting for their share of the pie. The changes that came with the Supreme Court's decision to eliminate 'separate but equal' schools [brought] challenging and exciting times for all Texas teachers. The two associations had to come together to consider desegregation. Strategies had to be worked out in order to move the merged associations into the mainstream without too much loss of identity . . .

"Contacts were, of course, important. There were teachers, both black and white, who encouraged my participation, and supported my candidacy financially, as well as volunteers. I was opposed by two males—one Puerto Rican, the other Anglo. Each of the candidates was respected and qualified to accept the position; however, I was better qualified and better organized. I entered the race as an urban candidate at a time when there was some resentment toward cities, which forced a runoff. During the runoff, the Puerto Rican candidate and his supporters joined my campaign and helped me win."

In 1984, the year in which Leontine Kelly was elevated to the rank of bishop in her church, it was a multiracial coalition of supporters which assured her nomination and selection.

CHAPTER 7

AGAINST THE ODDS: AFFIRMATIVE ACTION AND THE BLACK WOMAN

"I started my insurance agency in the den of my home. Because of affirmative action, I received my first large insurance contract in 1970. I was the first woman to receive a contract of this kind with the City of Los Angeles. That paved the way for other businesses headed by women to compete for municipal contracts. President Johnson was giving money to the cities in his War on Poverty, and Los Angeles received sixty million dollars to create programs in the Watts area, where there had been a riot, and in the East Los Angeles area, where there is a large Hispanic population. Because my company qualified to write the entire insurance program and specifications, this was a real turning point for my business. In those days, women were not in insurance except as underwriters." —IRIS RIDEAU

IRIS RIDEAU was born in New Orleans. "There was not a great emphasis placed on education in my community, especially with Creoles. Both my father and my mother attended high school, but neither graduated. Although he left school when he was a teenager, my father came to realize the importance of an education and encouraged me to stay in school and attend college. My mother, who was quite young when she and my father separated, could not see nor advise me beyond hard work and marriage, the only life she knew. In fact, I did not get direction until my second marriage, at the age of nineteen. I was motivated by my new husband's encouragement. He was a person I respected, so I accepted his guidance."

In her early fifties, Rideau looks a young forty, which she says is the result of a disciplined health regimen, meditation, and keeping a positive attitude about life. Her investment company, located in an upscale industrial park in Culver City, California, gives testimony both to her oriental philosophy and her talent for decorating. Each area in the suite of offices creates a mood of gracious welcome and a feeling of well-being for her clients.

Rideau's life was not always so fine-tuned. She recalls being confused and rebellious in her teen years. Her mother had very few parenting skills. When they moved to Los Angeles and settled in one of the projects in Watts, Rideau became pregnant at fifteen. "I was sixteen when I had my daughter. The boy I married lived near me, so we lived together until I left him and returned to my mother." Rideau hadn't anticipated the difficulty of marriage and a child. "Caring for my daughter was a long, drawn out challenge . . . without my mother's help, I could not have done it ."

After her child was born, Rideau worked in a factory during the day and went to school at night. "Because I worked during the day, I received my high school education through an adult education program. Factory work held no interest for me, so I enrolled in a trade school to learn to be a PBX operator. Actually my dream was to become an interior decorator. Toward that end, I took interior design courses at UCLA.

"I didn't complete my design courses, because I had to make money to take care of my daughter. I reluctantly left school to find a job and was hired by an insurance company to work as a PBX operator and a receptionist."

Rideau had no idea at the time that the receptionist job would be her initial step into a fulfilling and highly successful career. She took classes on insurance subjects, making herself eligible for promotion. "It did not take me long to realize that insurance and finance would be my career choice. I also realized that I wanted to be my own boss."

Rideau's success was not achieved without challenges. She explained that in the investment business, firms such as the Solomon Brothers,

Prudential-Bache, Dean Witter, and the other major competitors function in a totally closed environment. Very few black women, if any, are allowed into the loop.

Rideau's company specializes in public financing, and she has worked with the city of Los Angeles' affirmative action programs for many years, trying to break down barriers. "It was difficult to get purchasing agents to open the doors to more women. It is a continuous struggle. We make progress on one level, and then we find there is another level to conquer . . . When you have advanced to a certain level, they tell you that you are no longer disadvantaged. My point is that as long as we are black, and as long as we are women in this country, we will be disadvantaged." Rideau argues that just because doors have opened slightly, there should be no restrictions based on previous success. She is totally against impending legislation that would abolish affirmative action. "Minority businesses owned by women must be allowed to grow as large as they are capable of growing. Convincing others of that philosophy is one of my projects."

When I asked Rideau if she thought that there was a correlation between her achievement and affirmative action, she responded, "Affirmative action was the grease that turned the wheel. It helped me and made it a lot easier for me to succeed—but I had the will to succeed. Everything that I decide to take on as a challenge, I succeed in." In trade school, where Rideau learned about office machines so that she could work as a receptionist, she was the best student in her class, and she was a straight-*A* student in her interior design class. "I am a 'self-motivator.' That is what has driven me to succeed, and that is what drives me today.

"Another motivator is the environment that I grew up in. I never want to experience poverty again. That is what drives me. Also, when my daughter was growing up, I wanted to provide her with the security that I did not have as a child."

Rideau chose a career in sales and services because of her love and respect for people. "In this business especially, it is important to be people oriented. One has to trust that the choices one makes are correct and will succeed . . . [A] person has to have the training, the ability, the persistence—a willingness to work, interpersonal skills, and a belief in oneself. You have to have what it takes, because affirmative action will only help you get a foot in the door; it will not assure that you will succeed ."

MORE PROS THAN CONS?

Affirmative action is an issue that touches the lives of everyone in America. Hundreds of thousands of women and minorities who have received an education and entered the workforce have benefited from its programs. The question of whether black Americans needed a hand, and continue to need a hand, in order to share fully in the opportunities offered all Americans is central to the issue. What is most frustrating to many women I spoke with is the beating affirmative action is taking by people who don't understand either the definition or the significance of the law.

On September 24, 1965, as part of his assault on poverty, President Lyndon Johnson signed into law Executive Order 11246, which required federal contractors to take affirmative action to remedy past employment discrimination. In 1968, Arthur Fletcher, President Nixon's assistant labor secretary and the highest-ranking African American in the administration, developed the first enforceable affirmative action plan. The plan required a federal contractor in Philadelphia to distribute a certain number of labor hours to minority workers. The Philadelphia plan, implemented throughout the country, required that all government contractors set timetables and numerical goals toward the recruitment, hiring, and training of minorities and women. Voluntary and court-ordered hiring and assistance were soon contained in the goals of government agencies, universities, and corporations.

It is a fact that women have benefited more from affirmative action than other groups. The inroads into education, the workforce, and business gave women opportunities that had been off-limits to them in the past. Women will also be affected most dramatically if affirmative action is revoked. At this point in time, white women are not just working to find themselves; the majority are working, like black women, out of economic necessity.

Affirmative action made it possible for many of the women I interviewed to pursue an education and a career that might have been unavailable to them otherwise; they don't want to see these gains lost for the next generation of American women.

Educator Jewel Plummer Cobb is concerned that pending legislation will only exacerbate the situation in fields such as math, science, and medicine, in which women have traditionally been underrepresented in this country. "Affirmative action says one must aggressively seek candidates. It does not say that you must hire them if they are not qualified. That is a very important distinction. When I say that I speak for affirmative action, I speak for aggressive recruitment. I speak for positive reasons for hiring. I speak for those qualified minority and female applicants who will provide and honor our students with outstanding credentials. These people can be an inspiration to others. They can be role models for the students. And they can bring to the campus another dimension, a heterogeneous dimension to the student population. Some white folks tend to make an assumption that affirmative action forces an inferior person onto the campus community. That is the problem of many whites. They tend to use the less-qualified tag as a weapon against affirmative action. It was never established for the purpose of hiring unqualified persons."

Cobb believes that her active involvement in the community, and service on several business, arts, and college boards, are important adjuncts to helping the cause of affirmative action. "I feel that it is important to serve on boards, which, in general, are policymaking bodies. As a board member, one has the potential to influence the policies of an organization, and this is true in a variety of areas, from schools and colleges to corporations in business and industry.

"If a corporation or organization selects a black person, it clearly makes a statement about the policies of that company. It indicates a strong feeling about the presence, employment, and advancement of minorities. Obviously, a black member of a board is going to be aware of that. Not so much to police, but to be aware of what is going on in the organization. When a woman is on a board, there is a question that must always be asked, 'What are you doing in the area of hiring women, particularly in the areas at the top?' So, the board member brings to the company a certain awareness."

NASA researcher and wunderkind Pat Cowings also benefited from affirmative action but sees problems with it. She believes that affirmative action has actually been a disadvantage for her. All it did was make her peers assume that she was less qualified than they were, whether at graduate school or in the workplace. "Fortunately," she says, "after twenty years, one aspect of my difficulties is beginning to be resolved—my youth. I have staff changes every few years. In the early days, it was rough, since I was heading a staff much older than me. I remember joking about that. Now that I am getting older, they seem to be getting younger. I used to say that being a scientist was one area where a woman can hardly wait for her first gray hairs to appear. You can wear them like a badge of honor. But now that the gray is coming in fast and furious, I have started using Miss Clairol on a regular basis."

Harriet Michel, president of the National Minority Supplier Development Council, told me that she came along at a time when being a black female was somewhat of an advantage. "We were the first generation of affirmative action. There was a different climate; people were at least making attempts at inclusion. There have been many times in U.S. history [when] I might have been excluded from employment opportunities, but when I entered . . . the workforce, the time was right. It was in the best interest of organizations where I worked to include me in important positions. So I benefited. When I hear people say that the programs in the '60s and '70s did not work, I offer myself as an example that many aspects of the programs did work. Every black person I know is a beneficiary, especially those in my age group. Opportunities were made possible because we were in an era of inclusion."

Affirmative action has also seeped into religion—not because it was required, but because, as Jewel Plummer Cobb told me, "It was the right thing to do." Leontine Kelly believes that women are beginning to share the power in churches. It was not so much an issue of the individual, but, as her election to the bishopric demonstrated, "It was time for a woman. It was time for an ethnic."

Eileen Norton has a different view. "Because I had such a difficult time convincing my high school counselors that my grades qualified me for UCLA, I was surprised to find so many black students with *C* averages attending UCLA. They qualified through the affirmative action program. Affirmative action did not help me; I entered UCLA on my own merits but was able to observe the program during my time there. The students in the program were tutored and paid to attend—really nurtured. As a consequence, there were a lot of minority students on that campus who started when I started but were not there when I graduated. At the beginning, you could walk around and meet lots of black students; then, suddenly, quarter after quarter, there were fewer and fewer on campus. By my senior year, I had to look for black students. It was weird. Many of those students in the affirmative action program did not make it, because UCLA was not the place to learn to be a good student. I believe the guidance and tutoring, good study habits, and learning how to write a paper have to start before you get to college. Even high school is probably too late. Much of what they were teaching those students needed to have begun in elementary school. That's the closest I've ever been to affirmative action. I knew that it existed, and I knew students that were in the program, but most of them vanished."

Like many of the women I interviewed, Dr. Lydia Pettis-Patton would have made it with or without affirmative action. The first black woman to head a municipal department in the city of Portsmouth, Virginia, Pettis-Patton is director of Leisure Services, a conglomerate of several divisions that include parks and recreation, museums, libraries, golf courses, and the bureau of conventions and tourism. She came to this position with experience as a teacher, counselor, and director of recreation for the city of Durham, North Carolina.

One of the first questions I asked Pettis-Patton when we met was whether being a black woman had given her an advantage. "I think being a black woman who is highly qualified, educated, competent, creative, and assertive has given me some advantages in my career. I'm a risk-taker. There are lots of women out there, and a lot are on the same track that I was on, but I don't think it was the color that made the difference.

If Oprah Winfrey did not have what it takes to be a television spokesperson on her talk show, Oprah Winfrey would be just another black woman among the masses of black women. She is, however, talented, has a gift for what she is doing, is polished, and has pushed and shoved her way into a niche where she can make choices and decisions which gives her more power and authority than Miss Whoever, who is sitting and waiting for her ship to come in. My ability to know that I can move mountains—in a moral and ethical way—if necessary, for my own good, for the good of my family and my community, makes the difference in my success as a black woman."

Pettis-Patton was born in Fort Lauderdale, Florida, where her father worked as a waiter, and her mother worked at home raising seven children. Growing up during the '50s and '60s at a time when people in her town had a great respect for teachers, her early childhood ambition was to be a teacher. "Teachers were looked up to; we put them on pedestals. In my early years, I admired my teachers so very much. As a child, my favorite game was to play school, either with my friends or alone in my room. Someone gave me an old class-roll, so, of course, I was the teacher."

Since her parents were poor, Pettis-Patton felt that the best way to be assured of a college education was to excel in high school. "I always had a desire to be better and to live better than what I experienced as a child. The conditions that we lived in as children were a strain to my parents. My father had to struggle to make a living as a waiter, since my mother worked only occasionally. My family believed that a college education opened doors to a better life."

In high school, she made good grades and was active in extracurricular activities. "Whether it was physical education, a science project, a club or organization or running for high school queen, I always tried to excel and be a leader in everything I did. I believe that this desire to achieve has always been with me.

"When I graduated from college, I achieved my childhood dream of becoming a teacher. I was hired as a classroom teacher in an inner city junior high school in Louisville, Kentucky, back in 1969. I was very supportive of my students, encouraged them—but I was also a strict disciplinarian. During that time, I received an opportunity to return to the University of Louisville to get a master's degree in guidance and counseling. It took a year and a summer to complete my master's. When I returned to the school system, I was assigned as a counselor at the senior high school. That was a significant move, because I was the youngest secondary counselor in the school system. It was an important advancement, since I was a young black woman with a master's degree but no experience in counseling. I did not know it then, but I was soon to start on a career track toward upper management. I left the school system to become the director of recreation for Durham County, North Carolina."

Pettis-Patton, who earned her Ph.D. in 1986, explained that people often put affirmative action and the black woman in the same category. She believes that, especially in the last ten to twelve years, affirmative action has become the scapegoat for many of the country's ills. "At one time, when we spoke of affirmative action, we spoke of women, blacks, and, to a lesser extent, Hispanics. I have problems with that concept. When I first came to Portsmouth, people joked that by hiring me, the city had fulfilled every requirement except the handicapped. I take exception to that. When the city manager hired me, he knew that he had chosen the best person for the job. If he also was able to satisfy affirmative action requirements, so be it."

PBS vice president Jennifer Lawson brought yet another perspective to the discussion. "I have resisted applying for positions where I thought affirmative action would be a factor," she confessed. "For me that would have been a blow to my self-esteem. I would rather be hired and seen in a situation where I got there because of my abilities and interest in doing the job, not because of the color of my skin or because I am a woman."

Jackie Tatum was first hired by the Los Angeles Department of Recreation and Parks in 1955 as a $1.50 an hour, part-time recreation center assistant. At that time, her immediate goal was to place high enough on a civil service exam to become a full-time recreation director making $500 a month. Tatum thought she would advance quickly through the system on her own merits, experience, education, ability, knowledge, high standards, and quality work habits; but this did not happen. Like many of the black men and women who worked with her, she soon found out that it was impossible to penetrate the deeply entrenched "old white boy club." It was not until affirmative action became a reality that serious efforts were made toward equal opportunity for minorities and women.

Tatum's chance came in 1970, five years after Presidential Executive Order 11246 was signed into law. After working for several years as a middle-level supervisor and taking civil service exams in order to be promoted, she was appointed to a district supervisor position. After that, her firsts began to multiply. She advanced to an area supervisor's position, and then became an assistant general manager. In 1992, following an international search for a new general manager, Tatum placed number one on a list of qualified candidates. Her appointment—which, she reminded me, was based solely on merit—put her in charge of 2,000 employees and a ninety-six-million-dollar budget. It also made her one of the highest-paid black women in the country.

With their successes, these women have turned legislative possibilities into social realities. "This social consciousness," publisher Ruth Washington told me, "will triumph over all who oppose it. The torch has been lighted and will not be extinguished, with or without affirmative action."

PART III
PROFESSIONAL PROFILES

Women should be tough, tender, laugh as much as possible, and live long lives. The struggle for equality continues unabated, and the woman warrior who is armed with wit and courage will be among the first to celebrate the victory.

—MAYA ANGELOU

CHAPTER 8

CAREER STRATEGIES

"Many of my dreams have been undone and redone a few times over, and I'm aware of the imprint these experiences have made on me, but I learned important lessons from each of my negative experiences as well as from my positive ones." —JACKIE TATUM

J ACKIE TATUM and I have been friends since the 1950s, when we both worked for the Los Angeles Department of Recreation and Parks as recreation directors. In those days, there were only whites at the top of the organization. The best we could hope to achieve were lower-management supervisor jobs, and we were happy to get those. I left the department to work in other areas, but Tatum stayed on, shattering the glass ceiling to become the first woman and the first African American to head the department in its 106-year-long history.

A youthful sixty-four, dressed in an attractive black and white suit, Tatum welcomed me into her impressive, plant-filled office—a far cry from the plain, utilitarian beige offices we both started out with.

"The road to this office was not easy. There were challenges and barriers along the way, but I was determined to be the best in my field. I have always felt that I could go anyplace and do an excellent job, but I chose to remain here. My self-confidence was enhanced by my parents, who made sure that I received a solid cultural, social, and educational foundation. My mother and grandmother were my first role models."

As a young girl growing up in Kansas City, Kansas, Tatum studied dance and drama and frequently went to concerts and the theater. Her summers were spent on university campuses, where all three—mother, grandmother, and granddaughter—enrolled in classes. "Although my mother and grandmother had college degrees, they felt that a process of continuing education was important for them . . . I am following that tradition, because I believe we have to keep up with what is going on, globally, socially, politically, and technically."

Tatum is proud of the fact that she grew up in a career-oriented environment, where education and achievement were respected, and both the men and the women of the family worked. Among her relatives were four teachers, a doctor, and a dentist. Her mother and grandmother had degrees from the University of Kansas. Her mother also earned a master's degree from the University of Southern California (USC). Because of the many credits she earned in summer school, Tatum was able to graduate from high school at fifteen. She then entered the University of Kansas, later transferring to USC.

I asked my old friend whether she was comfortable with her success. "I always felt that if I were to survive in my career, I had to feel comfortable with myself. You know, have a sense of self, which I have always had. I credit my parents for helping to establish a soft but resilient shield that has been my armor in many situations. Give me an equal opportunity, or even close to equal, and I will succeed."

BETTER THAN AVERAGE

Most black women would agree that it's difficult to break through the glass ceiling. However, as many of the women I interviewed have shown, it is not impossible. The ones who have met the challenge know that they can't rest on their laurels. Highly visible, they cannot afford to make serious mistakes. Creative and assertive, they must also be able to function as part of a team. Assumed to be nonthreatening, they must not be afraid to make unpopular decisions. For the most part, they know that they have to be better than their white counterparts—one step ahead—just to stay even.

Faye Washington is assistant general manager for the Los Angeles Department of Water and Power, one of the richest and most influential municipal departments in the nation. In 1968, when she first entered the city workforce, she was determined to rise from her entry-level clerical position to the top echelons of the organization. "I began as a senior clerk and [was] promoted rapidly through the series. My primary strategy was to quickly learn the rules of the game, and how to play by those rules. I knew that I had to be better than the next guy. I also had to be trustworthy and become part of the team. In order to advance, I had to take civil service exams and pass high enough to be interviewed. I became a jack-of-all-trades, the consummate generalist, technically expert in some things, but having knowledge in many areas on a number of levels." When Washington was appointed general manager for the Department on Aging, she became the first African American female in the history of Los Angeles civil service to hold a position of that rank. In 1994, she was appointed general manager of the city's personnel department; and, in October 1995, she was appointed second-in-charge of Water and Power.

Washington was the twelfth child in a family of thirteen children, born in Beaumont, Texas. She grew up in San Bernardino, where her father was a minister who later became a bishop in the Church of God in Christ. "My father, a leader in his church, was highly respected in the community. When I was growing up, I had a respectful relationship with my parents. They were from the South, and as a result our home life was very disciplined. Our relationship was quite open, because I could communicate with them. They responded to my opinions. Although my father is no longer with us, this relationship continues with my mother."

Washington's parents motivated her to get ahead, instilling in her a strong desire to achieve. "More importantly, my parents taught me to think for myself. They taught me to plan for myself and not allow others to dictate the direction of my life. My mother taught me patience, and she taught me prayer. I felt a tremendous responsibility to succeed because I knew my parents had faith in me, no matter what course I took.

"As a child I placed more [pressure] on myself than anyone would dare place on me. I was president of my organizations—I never wanted to be secretary. I sang the loudest in my choral group so I could be lead singer. I don't know if it came from being a preacher's daughter. You know, having the entire congregation looking at you to see what example their minister is setting. I always felt a certain spirit within that has guided me in a particular way . . . Although my life was structured at home, I was able to show my parents ways of doing things differently. It probably contributed to my skills as a negotiator and debater. I was a debater in college—perhaps that helped."

Although Washington encountered many challenges at the beginning of her career, she was able to overcome each of them. "The major challenge was getting into departments that gave me the experience I needed. I recall early in my career that I competed for a principal clerk position in the city council's chief legislative assistant's office. I did not get that position, perhaps because I was a woman, or perhaps because I was black. But things began to change, and a few years later I came to that office as the assistant chief legislative analyst in charge of the entire city council office staff.

"A personal challenge was my desire to return to college. I felt that the lack of a college degree was a minus. I had the ability, I had the knowledge, I had the intelligence, and I had the will. I was very well read, but... the lack of a degree was a negative, a deficiency in my personnel file. I knew that I had to return to school. A little voice kept repeating, 'Faye, return to school! Faye, stay in school!' It was a tremendous challenge to have to work, to go to school, to raise a family, and to maintain a marriage. One has to be a superwoman, so to speak . . . But having conquered that challenge, I consider myself very fortunate, or should I say blessed.

"I wanted a college degree for my own feeling of accomplishment . . . By the time I received my degree, many of my professional goals had been met. I was comfortable with my level of achievement. I did not use education as a benchmark to get from A to B; I used education as a process of learning, so I could do a better job. Professional development is important. Education and learning are lifelong commitments. When I was a legislative analyst assigned to work on a labor relations committee, I suddenly realized I knew little about personnel and labor relations. I immediately enrolled in labor relations and public sector negotiation classes at UCLA. And several years ago I completed a senior executive program at the Kennedy School of Government at Harvard. It was something I wanted to do.

"Although the city has been good to me, I don't need to be reminded where I came from. I never hesitate to provide support for professional development programs. Each time I give a workshop or speak at meetings and conferences, I get as much from the sessions as do the participants."

SMART MOVES

Faye Washington is an excellent example of a woman who made smart moves. Aleta Carpenter agrees with Washington's views on the desirability of strategic career planning. "Strategizing is especially important when you are thinking about a career or making a career move. I use some aspects of this process on a continuing basis. When I am planning a career move, first of all I find out if the career of my choice has current work value, and if I am willing to put in the time, expense, and hard work necessary to qualify for the job I want. If the answer is yes, I go forward toward my goal.

"At the beginning of a job search, I think about how the pieces will fit into a particular position. Before deciding on the job I want, I think about how I want to dress. Do I want a job where I can dress up every day, or do I want to wear jeans? Do I want a job where I interact with people, or do I want to push paper? I think about whether I want a day job or a night job. Do I want to work weekends? I think about what my needs are, and then set them down on paper. I go to the library and research those big books that tell you about the types of jobs available. If I don't know anyone with a direct connection, I network. I'm not afraid to ask. I did that when I started to model, early in my career; I did that when I went into radio. The feeling of entitlement really helps. When you feel it is right for you, you can make it happen. I don't want to sound like a mystic, but I have visualized in my mind every job and every career I've ever wanted, literally down to the building I wanted to work in. From time to time I take a personal inventory. It is important to take a mid-term inventory and another at the end of the year, of what I like about myself and what needs adjustments, what I did to better the organization and what I can do better."

Carpenter believes strongly that we have to define and set realistic goals. The goals may be a little beyond the reachable, but not so far beyond that it becomes a stress factor. When that goal is achieved, then move to the next level. While achieving her own goals, Carpenter reaches out to help others. "I try to make people aware of their own possibilities. No matter what age, race, sex, physical condition, or circumstances, dreams, and goals are attainable. The important thing is to go for it."

Carpenter gave her first two jobs as examples. "Since I was tall, I thought that I could become a model. Silly me—I didn't know that you had to go to a modeling agency. I simply went to a large department store and applied for a modeling job." Instead, Carpenter was hired as a clerk in the legal department. She took the job to help pay household bills but aspired to something better. One day she checked out the store direc-tory, and found out where the fashion buyers were located. She also dis-covered where they ate lunch. "I would take lunch the same time as they. I drank lots of tea, since oftentimes I couldn't afford lunch. After several weeks, one of the buyers noticed me and asked if I modeled. I was hired as a fitting and showroom model. At one of the bridal shows I modeled a beautiful wedding gown. The chance to wear a wedding gown was quite exciting, because when I married I could only afford a plain white suit . . . I later became a public relations specialist for Arnelle of California, a fashion design and manufacturing company in San Francisco."

After several years with Arnelle, Carpenter left to become a proba-tion officer and juvenile hall counselor. "I had wanted to be a probation officer since I was twelve. Where I lived, many of the men were continu-ally getting arrested. Most of them complained about their probation offi-cers, and I saw this as a way to help my community." When she decided to make her teenage dream a reality, she knew she had to get a college degree. "While in college, I volunteered to serve an internship in the probation department, because I wanted to make sure that this was the career I wanted. After a while, they began to forget that I was not being paid and accepted me as one of them. In fact, while I was still in college, they thought I was so good that they let me substitute my years of school and my volunteer experience for the four years required to become a probation officer."

Carpenter stayed with probation as long as she thought she was making a difference; but eventually she found that her way of making a difference was not the department's way. Especially in the jails, supervisors disapproved of her methods and placed barriers in her way. For her attempts to implement more humane treatment for the women inmates, she received written reprimands. "I felt that the pushing of food trays under the doors for the women was treating them like animals. I refused, especially when we were in a controlled area. Instead I would unlock the doors, and we all sat on the floor and ate together. I knew that I could protect myself if someone tried to escape."

While working in the penal system, Carpenter created several innovative changes. She badgered department stores in the area and received donations of cosmetics and hair-care products for the women. She taught them how to do manicures and pedicures, how to put on make-up, and how to style their hair.

"I instituted and led rap sessions. The women talked about men, pregnancy, and other subjects of mutual interest. The inmates began to open up and share their thoughts with the group. There was less violence, because the women began to develop respect for themselves and others. My male coworkers thought that the program violated policy . . . [E]ven though the program worked, I was prevented from continuing. Where I worked, the men were downright petty. Some of them would not speak or say hello to me. It was hard for females to get promotions. I gave it my best efforts, but since I was a threat to the system, I lost and left."

Carpenter's story reveals several important keys to success: know what you want in a career, go after it, but know when to cut your losses and leave. After leaving the probation department, Carpenter became a successful radio personality and worked for several years as president of a popular radio station in Oakland, California. Three years ago, she experienced what many highly paid executives are experiencing in today's job market—corporate takeovers and downsizing. The station changed ownership, and Carpenter lost her job. However, this temporary setback didn't stop her. Carpenter has started her own community development consulting business, and all signs show that it will be a great success.

CHAPTER 9

BLACK WOMEN AND THE ARTS

"I spent many hours in the library, and I read everything I could find on the craft of writing and on marketing your work. I had read during my search that every writer gets rejections . . . [W]hen I received rejections, it stopped me at first. But I started again, and in 1962 my first work, a poem. . . , was published."

—ELOISE GREENFIELD

AWARD-WINNING children's book author and poet Eloise Greenfield has always been an avid reader, but the desire to write only came to her later in life, after she had run across some articles about the craft of writing. She wrote three short stories, sent them out, and got three rejection slips in the mail. "I knew nothing about marketing my work or the craft of writing, but I had a feeling for it. I sent my stories out as a test, to see if it would work."

Between her first rejections and her first published work, Greenfield married, had two children, and held various jobs. A son was born to her in 1951, a daughter in 1958. During that period, her desire to write remained with her; she knew that she had to try again. In 1960 she resigned from a clerical job at the U.S. Patent Office to write full-time.

"At first I wrote whenever possible. Then I began to drop nonessentials in my life. I balanced my personal needs with the needs of my family. Both my . . . husband and my children encouraged me. We joked about our unique arrangement. There were times when I would say, 'I'm part-time mother today.' My children knew that I was there for them to discuss problems, but I was not there for extra activities, such as taking them to the pool or having their friends over. Many of my family responsibilities remained whether I wrote or not, but the pressure was lessened. One of the things I did was put up a screen in the dining room for my office. The children knew that they could come behind that screen anytime; but that day, I was a writer, not a full-time mother."

Greenfield began to sell her work to newspapers and small journals; no publication was too small. Every accepted work was both a triumph and a source of encouragement. Feeling a need to be with other writers, in 1971 she joined the Black Writers Workshop of Washington, D.C. "When I first started, I was more interested in experimenting with various writing styles—I had neither a specialty nor a focus. It was during discussions at the Workshop about the lack of children's books portraying African Americans that I decided to focus on writing books for children."

Sharon Bell Mathis led the children's literature section of the Black Writers Workshop. Greenfield found the group very helpful. "We discussed each other's work and made critical suggestions." Mathis suggested that Greenfield write a biography and submit it to Crowell Publishers, which was looking for stories of historical or popular black figures. Mathis was working on a biography of Ray Charles, and another writer in the Workshop, Ophelia Settle Egypt, was working on a biography of James Weldon Johnson. Greenfield chose to write about Rosa Parks. "*Rosa Parks* was my second book. My first, *Bubbles*, was . . . accepted for publication in 1972. It had been rejected ten times before Drum and Spear Press accepted it. Drum and Spear was an African American publishing house in D.C."

Greenfield believes that there are too few African American publishing houses. "During the '60s and '70s, there were many active companies in this field. Many of the houses have since closed because of high operating costs. Also, most of the African American companies that are operating do not publish children's books, which causes a serious shortage of books about African American families."

Black Butterfly published Greenfield's popular book, *Nathaniel Talking,* and is publishing several other books written by her with Jan Spivey Gilchrist as illustrator. Gilchrist illustrated *Nathaniel Talking* and *Children of Long Ago,* a book of poetry written by Greenfield's mother, Lessie Little.

Even though Greenfield has now published more than twenty books for children and won numerous awards, writing has never become a matter of routine or complacency for her. As she starts each new book, she says, "It's scary. I worry throughout until I get to the end—maybe it won't work. Fortunately, this hasn't happened; but when I'm writing, there is always that fear."

JOYFUL SOUND

Singer Henrietta Davis Blackmon began her music training in junior high school, when one of her teachers encouraged her to play a stringed instrument. The instrument she chose was the cello, which she continued to play until a teacher in high school encouraged her to concentrate on her voice, and to get further classical training. "She thought I sang better than I played." Following the teacher's advice, Blackmon's parents engaged a voice teacher from the San Francisco Conservatory of Music. While still in high school and college, Blackmon performed with the Choral Society of San Francisco and the San Francisco City Choir.

When I asked her if anyone else in her family had musical talent, Blackmon explained that everyone in her family was musical. "My oldest sister Grace does a lot of gospel singing in the Detroit area, in New York, and in New Jersey; she works often with the National Baptist Convention and the National Baptist Congress and teaches at some of their Congresses. My sister Carolyn is also talented. My mother sings and has always played piano at various churches. She continues, even now, to play the piano for the children's choir in the church she attends in Detroit. My father played a little bit, and my brother Henry, Jr., also sings. When my father died in 1984, my brother succeeded him as minister."

Born in Detroit, Blackmon was the youngest of three daughters;

Henry Jr. was the baby of the family. Both parents were born in Mississippi, her father in Dodgeville, and her mother, Ouida Davis, in the Summit-McCone area. Reverend Davis moved his family to San Francisco when Blackmon was a sophomore in high school. She finished high school in San Francisco, earning her bachelor's and master's degrees at San Francisco State University.

Blackmon's first professional audition was in San Francisco for a role with the Metropolitan Opera. Twenty years old at the time, she discovered that she was the youngest singer at the audition. "During the competition, my mother, who was sitting in the audience, became so excited when it came my turn that she jumped up, accidentally hurt her knee, and was taken to the hospital. I did not win, because of my youth, but I auditioned again the next year and won. I then went to Los Angeles and won again."

In 1978, soon after graduation from college, Blackmon became a professional singer, specializing in operatic and classical music. "About that time, the Houston Grand Opera came to San Francisco, and a teacher suggested that I . . . audition for a part in *Porgy and Bess*. I went to see the show and thought it was great. I inquired and learned that they were looking for someone to play the role of Clara, Jake's wife. Clara is the one who opens the opera with a baby in her arms and sings 'Summertime' . . . I auditioned, and to my delight I got the part. We went on tour for six months." When the tour ended, Blackmon returned to San Francisco and performed locally until the opera went back on the road. She then joined the opera in Europe and spent six months on tour in several countries. Shortly after returning home, Blackmon again was selected and traveled with the opera, this time to Brazil. "*Porgy and Bess* has been good to me," she said.

When Blackmon is not performing in operas or giving classical concerts, she works the religion circuit, performing in such concerts and music festivals as the Praise-Sing Festival held in Nashville. Since her father was a minister, and she grew up in the church, gospel music has been an important influence in her life. She sees gospel and classical music as the best of two worlds. "I can do sacred music and I can do highbrow classical stuff. It works out to my advantage."

Blackmon explained that a singer has to be careful about being typecast. "You don't want to be in a position where it's thought that you can only do black productions. You can be typed as a background singer, or a member of a chorus, which makes it difficult to become a solo artist. Unless you are a Leontine Price, a Jessye Norman, or a Kathleen Battle, . . . it is inherently difficult. Many well-known black artists first attained fame in Europe before they were recognized by audiences in America."

Recently Blackmon began to sing voiceovers for commercials to supplement the income from her other engagements. "I was singing at an event in Beverly Hills when a young woman came up to me and asked if I were interested in doing commercials. When I told her that I was *very* interested, she gave me her card and told me that if something came up she would give me a call. Two weeks later she called and said that she had a commercial that I might be interested in. I went in and did it without an audition."

Because of the uncertainties connected with the performing arts, Blackmon cautions young people who are interested in performing to have something else to fall back on, whether a college education or technical training. Young singers need to have skills that can earn them an income between engagements. "Since I am paid substantially for some engagements and very little for others, it was important that I saved for the rainy days . . .

"Singing is what I love, and I would sing for free if I could afford it."

EVERYTHING OLD BECOMES NEW AGAIN

For a decade or more Betye Saar has been known for her elegantly composed assemblages created from recycled materials. You don't merely enjoy Betye Saar's artwork: to be in its presence is to experience its power.

Saar says that she inherited her artistic abilities from her parents. Her father was a poet, a writer of short stories, and an accomplished pianist. "My father found joy in playing the piano and writing, while mother enjoyed making things with her hands. Both were talented in their own way, and we kids grew up in an atmosphere of art and music."

One of Saar's important childhood memories involved visiting her paternal grandmother in Watts, California. There she attended prayer meetings at the Baptist church, where she enjoyed listening to the gospel singing. She also had her first encounter with a fascinating group of towering structures made out of bits and pieces of bottled glass, colored tile, and cement—the Watts Towers, built by Simon Rodia, one of her grandmother's neighbors.

After graduating from UCLA in 1949, Saar was employed as a social worker. The turning point in her life came when she met artist Curtis Tann, an accomplished copper enamelist and veteran of Caribou House, a Cleveland, Ohio, settlement house founded under the Work Projects Administration of the Depression era. Tann helped Betye Saar put her work before the public, and introduced her to many artists—Tony Hill, Wilbur James, William Pajando, and others who had moved from the East in the 1950s to settle in Los Angeles.

In collaboration with Tann, Saar designed and produced enameled art pieces, which they sold at gift shows. At one of these shows, she was introduced to an artist named Richard Saar, who owned a ceramics business and exhibited his crafts near their booth. She and the artist began running into each other at social functions, and developed a close friendship. Their marriage followed soon afterwards. With the birth of their three children, Saar left her job in social work to stay at home. "By then, I had gotten into printmaking and other related work. It was about this time that I began to experiment with and combine materials, moving . . . into new and creative art forms."

During those early days, Saar became intrigued by the assemblages of Joseph Cornell, an innovative artist from New Jersey who created three-dimensional montages encased in boxes. Saar began to create art assemblages that reflected Cornell's conceptual influence but were imbued with her own spirit and vision. Her work is now exhibited in museums and galleries throughout the world.

Saar explained her philosophy in the exhibition notes for "Connections," a brochure created for a 1988 cultural presentation in New Zealand of her site installations and assemblages. "Metaphysical and ethnic references are apparent in most of my work. I have always been intrigued by the cultures of Africa, Egypt, Mexico, and Oceania. The concept of power displayed in African sculpture influences me as well. I interpret power as intuition, ancestral memory, personal experiences, dreams, feelings, and energy. The recycling of materials gives my work power by changing and reinterpreting the [uses for which materials were intended]. My artistic incentive is to create an aura of beauty and mystery."

Even though the biggest challenge for many artists is getting their work exhibited, Saar says that "all my requests to exhibit have come to me." She began exhibiting in open competition in 1965, at an All City Art Festival at Barnsdall Park in Los Angeles. While her work was on display there, a gallery owner invited her to show at his gallery. Another time, a gallery dealer from New York offered her a show merely on the basis of a set of slides. "My first big leap was in 1970, when the Whitney Museum in New York showed one of my pieces. A few years later, they gave me a one-person show. People see my work and invite me to show at their gallery or museum."

Saar is also in demand at universities and colleges and in earlier years taught art classes regularly. She now accepts only visiting teaching positions, because they offer opportunities to travel to different areas of the world, where she is able to collect materials for use in her work. She says that she is always on the alert for ordinary, discarded objects—beads, old photographs, broken dolls. "There is a treasure-trove of materials out there. My teaching trips give me an income and a chance to find materials that I can turn into art."

Saar makes a statement with her art that goes beyond mere esthetics. Through her designs and choice of materials, she tries to address larger questions. We were speaking together in her Laurel Canyon home when she pointed to one of her art pieces. "The box and the doll were thrown away. These discarded articles from Mexico and India represent different religions. It does not matter if you're Hindu or Muslim or Christian. The emphasis is on the coming together of many cultures as one unit."

When I asked about her dreams for the future, Saar thought for a moment and answered, "I'm a person who lives pretty much in the now. And right now, I'm dealing with the construction outside." I had seen the telltale signs of work going on when I'd walked up to the house. "But that construction brings me a reward. It will bring me a new garage for security, and it gives me a larger studio. The studio I have now is smaller than I'd like. I work small because my space is small. The large pieces I do on site at the museums and galleries. I want to see what happens in a larger space. I have lots of ideas, but I have had to confine these ideas to small things because of space restrictions. Perhaps the work will get larger. Large works are actually lots of small things put together and spread out."

Saar's three daughters are carrying on the family tradition. Lezley and Alison are both artists, as well as mothers, and Saar's youngest daughter Tracy is a writer. "After my daughters finished college, my life became my own. Just the personal satisfaction of making art is heightened. You see, I became a single mother when my daughters were young, so I experienced the challenge of rearing my girls without a full-time father."

Family is important to Saar. One of her goals is to create a family complex that will nourish and give support to her extended family. "My grandchildren are very important to me. When I think of my grandmother and her influence on me ... Well, I realize that, hey—I've got a job to do also. It is more than buying my grandchildren gifts. Sometimes it's spiritual nourishment, sharing whatever beliefs I may have. It's encouragement and telling them that they have value and are important to the scheme of things; that they are beautiful and perfect. I look forward to more of those moments and also many productive years of creating."

PHILANTHROPY AND THE ART OF COLLECTING

Eileen Norton and her husband, Peter Norton, are founders of the Peter Norton Family Foundation, which supports the arts, child welfare, human rights, women's issues, and the struggle to eradicate illiteracy. The foundation contributes funds to the Whitney Museum in New York, the Armand Hammer Museum, the Los Angeles County Museum of Art, and other museums throughout the country. Social and educational organizations such as the NAACP, the Negro College Fund, the Children's Defense Fund, and various AIDS projects also receive funds from the foundation.

When I arrived at the Norton home, the butler led me into a sun-drenched room that I would call a combination solarium–art gallery, looking out over a tree-filled ravine with a view of the Pacific Ocean. The banks of the ravine were awash with brilliant color: red and lavender bougainvillea, luscious green ferns, flowering jacaranda trees, hibiscus bushes, fuscias, deep purple cyclamen, and sea lavender. As far as the eye could see there was beauty. When I turned my attention indoors to the room I was standing in, there was beauty of a different kind. Natural light poured through the wide, spacious windows, illuminating the paintings on the walls and the sculptures on their pedestals.

In a 1994 *Los Angeles Times* story, Norton's husband Peter was quoted as saying that American wealth has three phases—making a fortune, using it, and dissipating it. He and his wife wanted their lives to encompass the first two phases.

The Nortons made their fortune in 1990, when Peter Norton sold his software firm, Peter Norton Computing Inc., for stock shares that sky-rocketed into a fortune worth over three hundred million dollars. Peter and Eileen met through personals ads they placed in the same issue of a Los Angeles singles magazine for career professionals. They are now in the felicitous position of being able to use their millions to fund good causes and lend much-needed support to artists who are either off-beat or just starting out in their careers. They recently were major supporters of an exhibition at the Whitney Museum in New York called "Black Male: Representations of Masculinity in Contemporary American Art."

"The foundation is a grant-giving institution that funds diverse cultural and humanitarian projects," Norton told me, flashing a dazzling smile that belies her basically shy nature. "My husband [and I were] involved in art collecting and philanthropy even before he sold his business. We decided to set up a foundation and to endow it so it would perpetuate our giving.

"My life now is totally different from what I ever expected it to be. As a child, I knew that I was going to college, because education was important to my family. My grandfather had what was equivalent to a bachelor's degree from Dillard University. When he was there it was known as Straight University. A college education was unusual for his generation. My oldest uncle graduated from UCLA and went to the Sorbonne. My mother had two years of college from Compton College, and my other uncle had several years of college. But when I entered UCLA, I had no idea what I wanted to do after college. I was not career-savvy. Since my uncle had gone to the Sorbonne in Paris, I thought that it would be great to major in French. My bachelor's is in French, and my graduate degree is in bilingual education. So what does one do with French? Well, after graduation, I could go into foreign service, or I could teach French.

"Someone told me about a program called English as a Second Language . . . [I]n order to teach the course, I had to go into a fifth-year credential program. Later, I started teaching English as a Second Language at an adult education school. I was there for a couple of weeks before being assigned to an elementary school." Eileen was working as a teacher when she and Peter Norton, who is white, started dating.

Norton's experience as a teacher has helped her understand the children's issues supported by her foundation. She serves on several boards concerned with child welfare and education, including the Children's Defense Fund. In 1993 she founded the Children's Forum. "The Forum was not planned," she explained. "It evolved from an educational issue that was developing in our community. A few years ago, in 1993, I read about plans to break up the Los Angeles Unified School District into smaller districts, and I became concerned. Having been a teacher, I was interested in knowing if a breakup of the district [would be] good for the district . . . or [whether it] would . . . be a disaster for the children of Los Angeles." In 1994, Marian Wright Edelman, founder of the Children's Defense Fund, was the Forum's keynote speaker. "Each year hundreds of people interested in children's issues attend the conference. In 1995, more than 200 heads of social agencies and interested community people attended the forum. [That year's] theme [was] 'Preserving Families and Protecting Children.'

"The foundation is interested in successful programs in the community that are helping children, whether it is AIDS babies, illiteracy, or after-school programs. That is my interest and my focus. The Forum plays an important philanthropic role at the foundation, because our mission is to help not only artists but also women and children."

The Nortons have a large personal collection of contemporary painting and sculpture. Since the time of our interview, they have moved from the mansion in Santa Monica canyon to a somewhat more modest home—an ostentatious lifestyle really didn't suit either of them. "Art was something both my husband and I were interested in even while we were dating. I was a teacher, and he was in computer programming, so neither of us had much money; in fact, our dating was mostly going to museums and art galleries. He lived in Venice when we met, so there were lots of artists around. We went to shows in the community and to studios and on gallery tours. It was something we enjoyed; we enjoyed meeting the artists. We frequently said that if we had the money, we would buy the art we enjoyed . . .

"[O]n one of our tours, we met this artist named Carla Pagliro . . . We kept telling her, 'Gee, when we get some money, we will buy something from you.' Then, one day, we suddenly realized that we had the money to buy one of her works." Norton smiled again. "That was the beginning . . ."

CHAPTER 10

TAKING CARE OF BUSINESS: BLACK ENTREPRENEURS

"In December 1970, when I walked into Ida Lewis' office, I told her if she gave me an opportunity, I knew that I could deliver what Essence *needed; that I would be the best beauty editor that* Essence *could hire. I had some background, but not what was needed for the position. My husband owned a beauty salon; and I owned a cosmetics company called Nequai, named after my daughter Shana-Nequai. I was an actress, and I had taught modeling at the Ophelia DeVore School of Charm. I convinced Ida that she should give me an opportunity. In retrospect, [I realize that] she believed in me because I believed in myself."* —SUSAN TAYLOR

SUSAN TAYLOR told me an abbreviated story of how she became editor-in-chief of *Essence* magazine. "I heard that *Essence* was looking for a part-time beauty editor and decided to contact the editor-in-chief, Ida Lewis, directly." A few weeks after their interview, Lewis telephoned Taylor, asking her to come to work part-time at a salary of $500 a month. That was in 1970, the year in which *Essence* was founded. "I am probably less self-assured and confident than I was twenty years ago," Taylor confided. "I believed that I could do anything then."

Her first assignment was to create a beauty and cosmetics story for *Essence.* The other editors, she recalls, surrounded her with assistance, helping her write her article on deadline and supplying the graphics. The article was the magazine's first about a beauty makeover with cosmetics and received an enthusiastic reader response. "After that first article, I worked very hard, and the assignments continued. In 1972, the magazine decided to make my position full-time, with the title of fashion and beauty editor." In 1981 she was appointed editor-in-chief.

Today, Taylor can look out her office window and see the building where, right out of high school, she had a job in the garment industry. "I was more interested in getting a job than going to college and accepted a receptionist job which paid $55 a week. My main interest was to become an actress, so I went to acting school at night. Soon realizing that I needed to earn more money, I enrolled at City College, taking night courses to brush up on my stenographic and typing skills. When I doubled my shorthand speed and increased my typing speed, the company doubled my salary. Within five or six months, I was making $120 a week."

Taylor believed that she was doing just fine. She had begun acting and about that time decided to get married. "My marriage gave me an opportunity to pursue my acting career more seriously. I did not have to depend on a nine-to-five job." She joined the Negro Ensemble Company, a foundation-sponsored theater group in New York City established to provide training, repertory, and employment opportunities for talented black actors. "I was not part of the premier group; the company maintained a second group for less experienced actors."

Auditions were a regular part of Taylor's routine. Soon she began to appear on television in walk-on roles with one or two lines. *As the World Turns* was one of the shows that frequently yielded work. Her acting career continued to grow, and she began to get better parts. "I understudied Paula Kelly in the *Dozens* on Broadway and made a film called *John and Mary* with Mia Farrow and Dustin Hoffman. The problem was that I did not feel satisfied inside. I began to realize that acting was not what I thought it would be. We tend to have an image of what a certain profession is like long before we understand its demands. I wanted to do something that I really believed I could be very good at, and acting was not it. I was not satisfied with my work, although I managed to get good roles."

Taylor and her husband also wanted to start a family. When she became pregnant, Taylor knew that she could not combine motherhood with acting. "As an actor, I had no control over my schedule, the hours I worked, nor the location sites. Some of the jobs were out of the city, so I decided to do something else."

Taylor enrolled in cosmetology school during her pregnancy, determined to eventually start her own business. After getting her license as a cosmetologist, she developed her own line of cosmetics. She called the company *Nequai,* which means "beautiful one" in Nigerian. Launched in 1970, the year after Taylor's daughter Shana-Nequai was born, Nequai Cosmetics was an immediate success. With her hair stylist husband, Taylor opened a shop in the Bronx called the Face Place, where he dressed and styled hair, and she sold her line of cosmetics.

"People told me that I wouldn't succeed, since I opened my business with so few dollars. I paid no attention to them, thank God. I went on to do what I had to do. I bought cosmetics bottles at a private label company and worked with several chemists to create the foundations for darker skin tones. The skin treatment and skin-care products already existed; these I bought and labeled. My entire investment in the company was returned within three weeks. There was a need and a demand for cosmetics that worked for African American skin tones, and I filled that need."

Although Taylor's business was succeeding, her marriage wasn't. She and her husband separated, and then were briefly reconciled before she decided to give up the marriage for good. Knowing nothing about her spousal rights, she believed her husband when he told her that if she left him, she had to leave the company, too. Nequai Cosmetics, with all its profits, passed out of Taylor's hands; but she got to keep her most precious "beautiful one," Shana-Nequai. Fortunately, by that time Taylor had begun working at *Essence.* "When I was first hired as beauty editor, I had several challenges: being a single mother was one, and the other was my job. I did not have all the necessary editorial skills. It was tremendously motivating, but also stressful. I had few opportunities to leave work and relax at a movie or have a meal with a friend. My whole existence was basically getting my daughter up in the morning, getting her dressed, and getting her to school. After that, I rushed to work and left the office earlier than anyone else, because I had to get to the nursery to pick her up. At the time, I was the only editor at *Essence* with a child. People did not have the sensitivity toward the needs of a single parent we have today. My life was very, very stressful." Ultimately, Taylor feels, the responsibility she had to cultivate as a single, working parent gave her the kind of self-discipline she needed to succeed at *Essence* and was a factor in her rise to the top of the organization.

Taylor believes that black women must respect who they are and constantly express admiration for what they have achieved, making the words "I love you, I celebrate you" their mantra and daily affirmation. "If we black women don't celebrate our own successes—if we don't give ourselves and one another our due—who will?"

ENTERPRISING WOMEN

Ruth Washington, born in 1914, was not the first in her family to run a successful business. Her mother was a caterer; one of her cousins ran a barbecue joint; another cousin, a female, owned several rooming- and boardinghouses in Kansas City that catered to railroad cooks, waiters, Pullman Porters, and black chauffeurs who could not stay in the downtown hotels with their employers.

Washington was of a generation in which many successful people received their education in places other than universities. She herself learned photography at the Metropolitan Business School in Los Angeles, where she became an expert portrait retoucher. After graduation, she and Norman Seminoff, a friend, opened a photography studio on Avalon Boulevard in Los Angeles. "We made everybody who came to us beautiful," she recalled. "We prospered because we were the only first-class studio on the East Side. Many black actors and entertainers came to us, as did the families in the community."

Unlike the confident professional who ran a successful photography business, Washington felt like a neophyte when she first entered the male-dominated newspaper business. The Los Angeles *Sentinel*, founded in 1933 by Washington's husband, Leon Washington, is a highly regarded daily metropolitan newspaper and a national landmark in the African American community. Washington took over its management when her husband fell ill with a massive stroke in 1948. Unprepared either by education or experience to take on the responsibilities of running a newspaper, Washington nonetheless faced the task squarely, learning as much as she could about publishing while simultaneously managing every aspect of the paper's operation. Washington dismissed the enormousness of her achievement. "That was the way I was brought up," she told me.

On Leon Washington's return some months later, Ruth Washington became the *Sentinel*'s business manager, filling this role until her husband's death in 1974. It was through Ruth Washington's initiative that the paper grew. The paper began as a weekly throwaway, housed in a tiny office just off Central Avenue on the East Side of Los Angeles. One of Ruth Washington's first initiatives in 1948 was to purchase a nearby building at Central Avenue and 43rd Street. "If we were going to grow, we needed more space. So I negotiated the purchase of the entire block for $25,000—a bargain in today's market. Mr. Washington started with eight workers; I increased it to forty-nine people." The Brooklyn Dodgers' move to Los Angeles, the Watts riots, and the assassination of Dr. Martin Luther King, Jr. were a few of the newspaper's historic headlines published while Ruth Washington was at the *Sentinel*'s helm.

"When I decided to take over for my husband, I knew that I wanted a newspaper that was respected by both the readers and the industry. I knew that white newspapers were the leaders in the industry, so each day I read many of their dailies and studied their format."

From the beginning, Ruth surrounded herself with the best staff she could find, hiring some of the country's brightest black writers. At that time, white-owned newspapers would not hire black writers, so she had the cream of the crop. To survive, Washington had to become overly organized. She designed personal memo pads and typed everything she wanted done for every department, personally communicating with each member. "I ran a hands-on operation. I was constantly dealing with writers, editors, reporters, photographers, circulation people, advertising executives, salespeople, bookkeepers—anyone who was pertinent to the operation. I know that 'micro-managing' is a dirty word, but that was how I managed in the beginning."

When the Washingtons were first married, they lived in Watts. Soon after, they moved to Pasadena. Because her husband wanted to get away occasionally to rest and relax, they bought a vacation home about a hundred miles away at Lake Elsinore. When Leon left the hospital, Ruth acquiesced to his desire to recuperate at their vacation home, which meant she had to travel two hundred miles each weekday to the *Sentinel.* "I would get up at six o'clock in the morning and be at my desk by nine. A young man was hired to care for Mr. Washington's needs while I was at the newspaper. My mother came to live with us and took care of our home in Pasadena."

The newspaper flourished for more than thirty years under Washington's careful administration and inspirational guidance. However, with the westward movement of blacks into integrated suburban communities of Los Angeles, the newspaper's circulation gradually declined. Early in the 1980s, Washington came to feel that the newspaper needed fresh new minds and management, so in 1983 she asked her long-time attorney, Ken Thomas, to take over as chief operating officer, while she continued on as publisher.

During our conversation, Washington frequently reached under her desk for a half-gallon plastic bottle of spring water, which she advised me to drink regularly for my good health. I had no idea that this vibrant woman would be dead from cancer a few months after our interview. She showed no signs of illness; her light brown eyes behind her oversized glasses were bright and witty, her near-white skin was flawless, her reddish-blond hair looked healthy, despite the fluorescent lights overhead, and her walk was brisk. She invited me to stroll with her around the neighborhood.

We walked south on Central Avenue. Mrs. Washington pointed out a small building half-hidden behind a giant drugstore. "That is where Mr. Washington started the newspaper," she told me. We crossed the street and walked toward the post office, which bore her husband's name. "The post office and the library are named after Mr. Washington." People on the sidewalk, at the post office, and at the library greeted her respectfully. Ruth Washington responded to almost all of them by name.

She led me to the north side of the *Sentinel* building, which boasts a colorful mural. Individuals depicted in the mural include Leon and Ruth Washington; Ralph Bunche, the former Undersecretary General of the United Nations and a UCLA graduate; former Los Angeles Mayor Tom Bradley; Councilman Gilbert Lindsay, Los Angeles' first black elected city councilmember; retired Congressman Augustus Hawkins; and jazz legend Duke Ellington, who frequently lived nearby at the Dunbar Hotel. Two slogans dominated the mural: "Don't Move—Improve," and "Don't Buy Where You Can't Work." Washington explained that the "Don't Move—Improve" slogan was fairly recent. Just as whites moved out of the South Central community in the 1940s, when an influx of blacks from the South moved into the neighborhood, many black homeowners in the 1980s and 1990s have left the area in response to the wave of Hispanic immigration. The second slogan: "Don't Buy Where You Can't Work" is a reminder of another time in the life of that community. It was the rallying cry during the '40s when Leon Washington and other black leaders organized a boycott against white-owned businesses that refused to hire blacks.

Returning to Washington's office, I took a last look at the many plaques and awards in recognition of the *Sentinel*'s journalistic excellence and of Washington's commitment to the community. They covered the walls of her office and were piled high on her desk, testimonials of the appreciation and respect felt for Washington by local and national leaders, social, civic, and professional organizations. She was a major fundraiser for the 28th Street–Crenshaw YWCA in Los Angeles and the cofounder, with Congresswoman Maxine Waters and Ethel Bradley (the wife of former Mayor Tom Bradley), of the Black Women's Forum. As our interview drew to a close, Washington leaned over and told me in a stage whisper, "I am the only person I know who has met Bonnie and Clyde, the bank robbers. It was while I lived in Kansas City." She leaned back in her chair again, her brown eyes sparkling. "But that's another story."

CONSULTING WOMEN

Dolores Ratcliffe, President of Corita Communications, Inc., was born in Los Angeles, the youngest of three children. Her parents met and married in Albuquerque, where her mother was born. Her father, born in Bowling Green, Kentucky, was voted valedictorian when he graduated from high school. "I think of my father as the scholar in our family," Ratcliffe told me. "He was a lover of books. After high school, he became an entrepreneur of sorts, involved mostly in barber shops." Ratcliffe's father told all his children, if you have a service to offer, you can always make a living. He encouraged Dolores' communications skills and entrepreneurial ability, while her mother encouraged her love for learning and the need to be independent. "In effect, I have sort of incorporated the interests of both my parents without even thinking about it. My mother had an interesting philosophy, which some of her friends shared: 'If you never learn to sew or cook, you will never end up in that kind of work.' So she discouraged that." Ratcliffe did not learn to cook until after she married, and she says with a kind of pride that she never learned to sew.

Even as a little girl, Ratcliffe wanted to be a teacher. She grew up to earn her bachelor's degree, a teaching credential, a master's degree from California State University, and a certificate in administration from Claremont Graduate School. Her special career interests were in communications, English, and Spanish. With her degrees and certification, Ratcliffe eventually was able to advance to top administrative positions in school systems throughout the Los Angeles area.

Ratcliffe wanted to teach secondary education at a time when most black female teachers in Los Angeles worked in elementary schools. In the 1960s, California had begun to enact laws and regulations mandating instruction in a second language for all students in public secondary schools. The resultant need for language teachers provided Ratcliffe with the career opportunity she was looking for. "They begrudgingly started me off in a junior high school . . . I was determined to work toward helping minority students."

After a few years, Ratcliffe left the Los Angeles school system to go to Pasadena, California. "My move to Pasadena turned out to be a wise move . . . I moved very rapidly up the career ladder. I was there only three years and was given an administrative position, which was unheard of—because I had not yet received tenure as a teacher."

Ratcliffe's lack of tenure presented some problems for other teachers. There were those who wondered, "How did she do that?" Actually, Ratcliffe explains, the principal at her junior high school, a woman, encouraged many women in the system, especially if she believed they had the ability to achieve. "Although I had been highly recommended, my immediate supervisor, a black male, told me that I was not his first choice. He told me that the only reason that he accepted me was because I had been highly recommended and . . . I was bilingual. He thought that since I spoke Spanish as a second language, I could appeal to a broader segment of the community." After moving into that same supervisor's job, Ratcliffe left the Pasadena school system to accept an administrative position with the Los Angeles County superintendent of schools. She later went on to work within the Culver City Unified School District.

When she left, after twenty-five years in education, to start her own business, Ratcliffe's challenges were more related to being a woman than to being black. "In business . . . they are quite concerned about your being a woman. I had been successful in getting around the [old boy] network in the school systems, so I used the same strategy as a businesswoman. I believe women creating their own network is one of the keys . . . "

I asked Ratcliffe if she ever felt a fear of failure. "Every time I go into a new role, I have a fear of failure. A new administrative post, new clients, training seminars, and so on—there is always that concern. In order to eliminate that fear, I go the extra mile of preparation . . . I overcompensate. Fear comes when you are not prepared, when you have not done your homework."

Recently she was invited to teach a business course at California State University at Northridge. She also assists nonprofit organizations and some for-profit organizations in obtaining grants and providing community programs on entrepreneurship. "I am on six boards, which may be five too many—but through these relationships, you receive business credibility." Ratcliffe warns that women should not join boards merely to sell their services or give their companies visibility: The primary reason for joining a board is to render service. "I've seen women make that mistake. They immediately start promoting their businesses, which is a strategic error. Also, I have noticed that men are chairpersons on the majority of boards. On the Los Angeles Industry Board, ... we developed a strategy of co-chairs, where some of the women would have positions of significance. [For three years] I co-chaired the grants and awards committee, a very powerful committee with a budget of more than thirty million dollars."

In 1984, Ratcliffe founded the Association of Black Women Entrepreneurs; she currently serves as its national president. "I want to help women, especially black women, understand the need to create and make money instead of just spending it as consumers. It is important that we understand the entire process of economics and its impact on our lives."

BUILDING DREAMS

Many years ago, Norma Sklarek and I were neighbors in Rustic Canyon, one of the beautiful and secluded communities in the Pacific Palisades area of West Los Angeles. Another neighbor, a talented artist, had invited me to her home to meet a friend of hers who also lived in the neighborhood. When I arrived, I was pleasantly surprised to see an attractive African American woman about my age, chatting with one of my neighbor's children. My neighbor had gotten us together because Sklarek and I were the only African Americans in our little canyon.

Since I was in a mixed marriage, I had felt a bit lonely, believing myself to be the only black person in the canyon. Sklarek was also in a mixed marriage and had felt the same way. My marriage did not last, but Norma remained married to Rolf Sklarek, an architect trained in Germany at the Bauhaus School, until his death in 1984.

Naturally when we met again for the interview, we had a lot of catching up to do. I had recently remarried, and so had she. At the beginning of the interview, all we talked about were our new husbands and the get-togethers we had enjoyed those many years before. When she went into the kitchen to make tea, I noticed she had done some remodeling; but the basic design of her home remained the same. Rolf had built their house more than forty years before. The Bauhaus-style structure, with its simple rectangular lines, high vaulted ceiling in the living room, and large windows looking out over the garden—Norma's prize-winning orchids and bromelia—was just as contemporary now as it had looked to me twenty years ago.

When we first met, I knew that Sklarek was an architect; but I did not know that she was the first African American woman to receive an architect's license in the United States, first in New York, and a few years later in California. Not only that, but Sklarek specializes in the large-scale architecture required for high-rises, shopping centers, and large building complexes—a particularly male-dominated architectural subspecialty in a field that is by and large dominated by men.

Born in Harlem and raised in the Crown Heights section of Brooklyn, Sklarek remembers spending her childhood working with her hands. She drew pictures of any relative who would sit still long enough. She decorated rooms and painted murals. She also painted and refinished furniture. One of her mother's favorite stories was about the first ten dollars that Sklarek saved as a child. Instead of buying a child's toy or a doll, she invested in a "How to Draw" book.

Sklarek's interests in high school were in the sciences. Her love of physics led her to believe that she would become a physicist. Since teachers were strong role models in her community, she had also wanted to be a teacher. However, her father, a physician, encouraged her to do something more exciting. He was the one who first suggested architecture to her.

Sklarek attended predominately white public elementary and high schools. Her drive to prove herself led to high achievement in most subjects, even those that did not particularly interest her. When she first graduated from Columbia, in 1950, twenty architecture firms turned Sklarek down before she was finally hired. "I could never figure it out. I don't know if the rejections were because I was a black person, because I was a young woman, or because of the economic recession at the time. Since I was turned down so many times in private industry, I went to work for the city of New York in a civil service job.

"I decided very quickly that civil service was not where I wanted to be. This inspired me to take the licensing exam as soon as I qualified. At that time, in addition to the academic degree, you had to have three years' experience. So I got the experience and quickly took the exam." Sklarek passed the entire thirty-six-hour exam on the first try—which was almost unheard of at the time. Most of her coworkers at the city were either unlicensed or had needed to take the licensing exam many times before passing.

Sklarek was expecting her second child when she left her job with the city. Later, when she was hired by a private architectural firm, she happened to meet a group of former coworkers from her old job. "When I told them that I was working for a certain firm, they were . . . shocked. They said, 'Shall we tell her? No, we shouldn't tell her.' I said, 'Tell me what?' Well, they told me they heard that my former supervisor had given me a completely negative recommendation. He said that I was lazy, that I knew nothing about design and architecture, that I socialized, and that I was late every day. These friends could not believe that I had gotten the job when they heard this.

"[I]f [my former supervisor] had been unhappy with my work, he could have had me transferred. The fact that I had worked with him all that time meant that he was satisfied. When the new employer asked if I had gotten along with my former supervisor, I said, 'Of course.' I guess he figured that nobody could be that bad. It taught me that it is possible to work next to somebody and not know that they hated you. It had to be personal. He was not a licensed architect, and I was a young kid—I looked like a teenager—and I was black and a licensed architect."

Sklarek's first assignments at the private firm did not at all capitalize on her talents—she was stuck with the boring jobs, such as drawing plans for the bathrooms in buildings. Later, when she was hired at a more prestigious architectural firm in New York, she made her new supervisor aware of her abilities. She let him know that she would not refuse to do bathrooms or other routine tasks, but she was capable of meeting considerably greater technical challenges. He wound up giving her so much work that one day he apologized for sticking her with all the tightly scheduled assignments. "[H]e told me, 'You are the only one that I can depend on to get those things done.' I was not aware that I was doing most of the difficult work."

Architects who had worked at the firm for twenty years or more began coming to Sklarek for advice on how to do certain jobs. She was puzzled that they asked her for help, but she would attack and solve these problems without revealing that she was facing most of them for the first time.

Sklarek had not planned to move to Los Angeles, but some friends encouraged her, arranging job interviews at various architectural firms. One prestigious firm she visited told her that they had never hired a woman architect before; they only had women as secretaries or decorators who chose paint colors. But they had no objection to hiring a woman now.

"When I moved a year later, I did not choose that firm. I chose the first firm I interviewed with, Gruen Associates. When I decided to leave Gruen, I went to the firm that said they had no objection to hiring a woman, and they gave me a very senior position as vice president. I was the only woman vice president they had. After I had been with this firm for about five years, I was having lunch with African American friends in the business. They mentioned that before I came to the company, the firm would not hire blacks. I refused to believe that and mentioned their comments to the architect who hired me. He looked me straight in the face and said, 'That's true.' So you see, people can change."

Sklarek feels that opportunities in her field are currently much better than they were when she first entered. "Women are making a greater impact on architecture than ever before. There was a time when many firms were reluctant to hire women and blacks." It was not until 1980, nearly twenty years after Sklarek was licensed in 1962, that the second black woman was licensed in California. Now there are several. One has gone into partnership with two other women, Sklarek told me.

"When my children were younger, they would get excited over the buildings that I was involved in. They did not care that those large, major construction projects were a team effort. They would say: 'That's my mother's project. My mother is the architect on that'—as if I had done those projects single-handedly!" Sklarek sat back in her chair. "I get a good feeling, too, when I see my work completed. I look forward to making a continuing contribution to architecture; and when I retire, I look forward to spending more time traveling with my husband." (Sklarek is now retired, and doing just what she'd looked forward to doing—traveling with her husband, playing golf, and giving occasional lectures on architecture.)

Sklarek's architectural credits include the city hall at San Bernardino, California; Terminal One at the Los Angeles International Airport; the Los Angeles Pacific Design Center; the United States Embassy in Tokyo; the Fox Hills Mall in Culver City, California; and South Coast Plaza in Orange County, California. Until her retirement, Sklarek was a principal partner at the Jerde Partnership, an internationally renowned architectural firm. In 1980, she became the first African American woman in the history of the Los Angeles chapter of the American Institute of Architects to become an AIA Fellow.

CHAPTER 11

EYES ON THE PRIZE: POLITICIANS AND PROFESSIONALS IN PUBLIC SERVICE

"My first political efforts taught me what this business is all about. The night before the official opening of our campaign office, somebody broke in and wiped us out. They took our office equipment, including typewriters that were borrowed. They took the peanuts, the drinks, and even the paper cups that were to be used for the opening day celebration." —STATE SENATOR DIANE WATSON

SENATOR DIANE WATSON'S district office is on Crenshaw Boulevard overlooking Leimert Park in southwest Los Angeles. Leimert Park is a popular gathering place for community meetings, political forums, and festivals. On the day of our interview, the senator pointed out a group of evidently unemployed young black men who were loitering in the park. The lack of jobs for men like those was one of her primary concerns, she told me.

Watson was elected to the California State Senate in 1979 for the twenty-sixth District of Los Angeles, representing more than 750,000 constituents. She was California's first black female senator and kept that distinction until former assemblywoman Teresa Hughes was elected to the State Senate in 1993. Watson explained to me that she had never intended to run for public office. "I was not interested in politics because

I had a lot of things going for me in education." In 1975, Watson became the first African American woman elected to the Los Angeles School Board; "I got into politics on a fluke." While Watson was working for the state-sponsored Allied Health Project at UCLA, a member of the Los Angeles School Board approached her, asking whether she would consider running for a position on the board. There would be people who would finance her campaign, Watson was told. The one catch was that she had to change her political affiliation from the Democratic to the Republican party. "That made me angry . . . I felt challenged and decided to file and run on my own."

The ransacking of Watson's headquarters seemed a minor incident compared to what followed later in the campaign. While waiting for the guests to arrive at the home of a well-known entertainer who had made her home available for a fundraising party, Watson received the devastating news that her campaign manager had been killed. That was the end of the line for Watson—she simply felt she couldn't go on with the campaign. A friend pulled her aside, hugged her, and said, "If you are going to be in this business, you have to learn to take the heat. Tom was working on your behalf. You cannot let him down. You are going to run, and you are going to win." Watson ran; and although she did not win that race, she won the next one, receiving over eighty percent of the vote. Her friend's death continues to haunt her even to this day.

When I asked Watson how she coped with the old-boy network in politics, she told me, "It's tough! What you have to do is overcome the barriers that are put in your way. Integrity is important. You break in by showing them that you can do the job as well or better than they. Slowly the door starts to open. But it doesn't open all the way, because white males do not consider you a peer when you are female and black."

She also believes in demanding respect. Soon after her arrival in the state capital, Sacramento, Watson gave a speech in which she explained that she was one-fortieth of the forty-member Senate and had been elected just like all the other members were. She assured her fellow senators that she did not get to the Senate on discount points or affirmative action, but in exactly the same way in which they had—by votes.

She also informed them that she had received more votes than anyone else running for the Senate in that election and that her constituents represented majority as well as minority groups. "I was not elected by black votes alone," she told me, "and I made my fellow senators aware of that fact."

Born during the '30s in Los Angeles, Watson was one of four children. Her mother, Dorothy O'Neal Watson, was reared in Chicago and came to Los Angeles when she was seven years old, via Oklahoma and Nevada. "My grandmother was a nurse at Provident Hospital in Chicago, but she wanted her children to be educated in the West. Although it took a few years, she was determined to get to California."

William Watson, her father, came to Los Angeles as a young man from his native Kansas City. A prizefighter, he wanted to be a world champion, like Joe Louis. "My father's trainer brought him to California, where he met my mother. That was the end of his boxing career and also the end of my mother's college education for a while. She had the distinction of being the third person to enroll at Los Angeles City College when it first opened. She returned many years later and graduated with my youngest sister."

Instead of pursuing prizefighting, Watson's father became a police officer with the Los Angeles Police Department. After distinguishing himself with LAPD, he was injured in the line of duty and took a medical leave. He never fully recovered, dying several years later from the lingering effects of the trauma. "I'm a policeman's kid, and, when I'm referred to as being soft on crime, I inform them that my father died from injuries received performing his duties as a policeman. I come from a family of policemen: My mother's brother was a police officer, and my cousin was the first black detective on the Los Angeles police force."

Before entering politics, Watson taught gifted children in Japan and France. While teaching in France, she was called back to the United States because of an uncle's illness. "He was the patriarch of the family and died upon my return. I had planned to leave my teaching assignment in France and go to a new assignment in Addis Ababa, Ethiopia, but soon after, my father . . . died. And right after that, my youngest sister got sick and almost died from cancer. It seemed that I would never go back; so I decided to return to school to get my master's degree."

Watson had received her undergraduate degree in education from UCLA. She earned her master of science degree in counseling and guidance from California State University, Los Angeles, and in 1987 earned a Ph.D. in education administration from the Claremont Graduate School. "After earning my master's degree, I received several offers to go into counseling. I worked as a school psychologist for about six months until a friend recommended me for a position at UCLA. There are people in our lives who are like our guardian angels. Every time this individual calls me, it is for some beneficial opportunity. He is always there for me and helped me shore up my courage to enter politics."

Watson devotes most of her time to addressing the needs of her constituents. She has authored numerous legislative bills geared toward improving the quality of life for people in the state. She also chairs one of the most important legislative committees in California, Health and Human Services, which oversees an annual budget of more than twenty-six billion dollars.

There's a good chance, with Watson's experience in Europe and Asia, that one of her other aspirations might become a reality: She has also dreamed of becoming a United States ambassador. Her first choice of countries would be Bermuda, where she has spent considerable time and knows the people well. Her second choice would be a Third World country, preferably somewhere in Africa. Watson is currently serving her final four-year term in the California Senate.

THE PEOPLE'S CHOICE

Echoing Diane Watson's words, Doris Topsy-Elvord told me, "Running for public office was not something I had anticipated. I had worked as a probation officer for twenty-seven years in Youth Authority and at Sybil Brand Institute, the Los Angeles County women's jail . . . In 1988 I retired at age fifty-five, after thirty-five years of service. I intended to stay home and rest, but the mayor of Long Beach drafted me to become a member of the Civil Service Commission. I did that for three years, then I was asked to run for city council against a person that I helped get in, but [who] had forgotten the people in his district. My predecessor, who had been on the council for six years, raised ninety thousand dollars for his campaign, and I didn't have one campaign dollar. I had to get out and raise money and, over a period of nine months, raised thirty-three thousand dollars with the help of thirty-five volunteers. We walked and talked and smiled and dialed and won the election by twenty-six votes. It was not about money. It was about focusing and working your plan. After that, success is yours.

"I did not want to run, but when you're called upon, you have to do what you have to do. So after I thought about it and talked it over with my husband and my family, I said, 'Why not me?' Someone has to do it, so why not me? Long Beach is a city that has eleven percent African Americans, so they can't possibly elect you alone. I've never felt any boundaries; I know that boundaries are there, but I don't acknowledge them. If you have the credentials and are prepared, there is no reason why you can't do it. If you're spiritual and the motive is right, it can be done."

During the nine months of campaigning, Elvord registered more than 900 people. "I went into pool halls, into barber shops, into places my predecessor would never have gone into. I registered unregistered and apathetic voters, the young people who had just turned eighteen, and people that others had forgotten. That's how I won. And to show you how tight the election was, during the primary, with just five weeks to go, my predecessor had 49.8 percent; I had only 30 percent. Five weeks later, I had 53 percent, and he had 48.8 percent. We won because we stayed focused, we stayed spiritual, and we knew our cause was just. We kept our eye on the prize.

"The council is made up of nine districts. When I first went on the council, there were eight Anglo males and myself. My strategy was not to be abrasive but assertive. I've long known that you don't have to have a gavel to be in charge. The person in charge is the person who has the best and most information. And I always try to make that person me. If I didn't have the best information, I acknowledged that; but whatever information I had, I shared. The other council members would often come and ask my opinion. I talk very little at council meetings. I do all my lobbying and talking before council, lining up the votes I need. With that method, I get whatever is needed for my district. I can never recall asking for anything that was not done. You have to know when to talk and when not to talk."

Born in Vicksburg, Mississippi, Elvord and her mother came to Long Beach when Elvord was in the third grade. "I was raised a Catholic. Ironically, even in Mississippi, I went to an integrated school, St. Mary's, which was the only Catholic school in town. The priests and nuns were Anglos, but the children were all colors.

"When we moved to Long Beach in the '40s, there were no black Catholics here. My mother attempted to get me into St. Anthony's School, but they didn't want me at St. Anthony's, because I was black. However, my tenacious mother did not give up; she went downtown to the Chancery in Los Angeles, spoke to Archbishop McIntyre, and got me into the school. For some reason, they gave me a test, probably to try and weed me out; but they forgot that I had come from a Catholic school, so I passed easily. At St. Anthony's, the entire school was white, but that was not a problem for me. It was normal for me to be among whites, since the nuns and priests and many of the students in Mississippi had been white. Since I did not have a chip on my shoulder, and the kids had not grown up racist, I never heard a derogatory word against me. I was treated with the greatest respect. In fact, I was deferred to. It was a most amazing thing. In retrospect I have to give my fellow students and their parents a lot of praise, because the kids had not been taught bigotry and bias as children, and . . . accepted me on face value."

Elvord's mother wanted her daughter to grow up in a multicultural environment. "My mother wanted me to be grounded in who I was and be with African Americans—otherwise I would have had no interaction with the boys and girls in my neighborhood. So I went to Catholic church at eight o'clock each Sunday morning and at ten-thirty went to the Baptist Church in my community to sing in the children's choir. I know both the cultures, and I have the ability to get along with all kinds of people. This has been a valuable asset. When I went to UCLA, I had a lot of Jewish friends and was invited to Passover seders in their homes. I have been involved with different cultures and religions all my life."

Elvord believes that women, especially black women, have to be supportive of each other and to encourage each other to reach out for whatever their dreams are. "We have to shoot for the moon, and, even if we miss, we will land among the stars. And we have to let our young people know that we are there for them; we can be resource people. I'm a resource person for many groups and for many people. I consider it a blessing, because the Lord allows me to do that. Sometimes it is very tiring, but I say, 'Why not me?' People have been there for me; now it is my time to be there for them."

Elvord helped organize the first midnight basketball league in Long Beach. "Except for the one in San Diego, we are the only league in Southern California. A great many people have come forward to help with the program. We have sixty young men who are no longer at risk. We have a 'fathers in the hood' program . . . It is federally funded to teach young males how to be fathers. Although our young fathers may not have jobs, or they may not live in the same house with the young mothers, they can change diapers, they can take their child to the park, they can read a story to their child, and, if the child is old enough, they can take them to sports events. Our young men can be fathers to their children, and I encourage their participation. Service to my district is my reason for being."

CRUSADING FOR WOMEN'S HEALTH

In 1969, when Vivian Pinn was completing her residency at Massachusetts General Hospital in Boston, a female student asked for her assistance in reviewing a set of slides. Twenty years later, that same student—Bernadine Healy—would become the first woman director of the National Institutes of Health (NIH). When it came time to select a director for NIH's new Office of Research on Women's Health, Healy recalled the intelligence and generosity of the resident who had helped her so many years before at Massachusetts General. Thus it was that Vivian Pinn came to leave her position as chair of the department of pathology at Howard University's College of Medicine to head the Office of Research on Women's Health at NIH.

Following her residency at Massachusetts General, Pinn had become highly respected for her research on women's and children's diseases. In 1982, when she went to Howard, she became the third woman and the first African American woman to chair an academic pathology department in the United States. In 1988, she was named president of the National Medical Association (NMA), a predominantly black professional organization founded in 1895, focusing on problems of health care access and professional education for African Americans. The eighty-eighth president of NMA, she was the second woman president in its history. A long-time advocate of women's rights to better health care, Pinn became interested in medical politics—particularly opportunities for blacks in medicine—while still in postgraduate training at Massachusetts General. "Although I belong to many medical organizations," she told me, "NMA is very special to me. It is an organization that allows its members to network with other blacks in the profession across the country."

In 1989 and again in 1990, Dr. Louis Sullivan, former U.S. Secretary of Health and Human Services, chose Pinn to serve as a member of the U.S. delegation to the World Health Assembly in Geneva; in 1990 she was elected to the Council of the International Academy of Pathology.

Pinn feels outraged that women have been ignored in most research efforts. Current studies on aging, heart attacks, and coronary arterial disease have either omitted women as subjects or included them only late in the protocol. One of Pinn's priority projects has been to create a unified strategy for exploring disease in women. "I want to help women scientists gain importance in the highest ranks of medical research in order to shape the research agenda that affects women's health issues . . . The 1985 comprehensive report from the task force on black and minority health found that the majority of deaths that occurred in the black communities were from cancer, heart disease, drugs and alcohol, diabetes, homicides or accidents, and infant mortality. These are diseases that can [in many cases] be prevented, treated, and cured. But patients must know there are services available to help them. Through organizations such as the NMA and NIH, we can make sure that all Americans have equal access to health care."

Despite her impressive array of achievements and honors, Pinn feels uncomfortable with the word *success*. She believes that she has not yet achieved many of her goals; there are still many gains to be wished for in the fields of health and medicine. "I don't feel I can sit back, thinking I have made it. I have a long way to go. I am still trying to meet these challenges. Still trying to do better."

Her dreams for her personal future are very modest. "I would like a night and day when I don't have to get up at the crack of dawn to do things. But then, if I didn't have the responsibilities I have, I don't know what I would do. I'm just looking forward to broadening my perspective and knowledge . . . in this new area of research. One of my missions is to make sure that women are not left out of nationally funded clinical trials. The Office of Research on Women's Health will continue to monitor the numbers of women and minorities in planned and ongoing research. We also want to make participation in clinical research more convenient for women, especially those with children, so that we can ultimately have better gender-specific and culturally sensitive medical care for women."

STAYING FOCUSED

It took thirty years and many careers along the way for Cynthia Shepard Perry to become a U.S. ambassador—but she never gave up and never lost sight of her goal. Perry was appointed by President Ronald Reagan as the U.S. ambassador to Sierra Leone, in West Africa; she was reassigned by George Bush to Burundi, a former Belgian trust territory of Rwanda-Uganda, in Central Africa. "An ambassador has the diplomatic responsibility to make sure that American policies are understood by the host government, and our government understands their policies. The ambassadors and their staffs must always present a positive picture of

America," Perry told me. In some cases, ambassadors also influence policy.

It was Perry's old high school principal who encouraged her to pursue her wild dream of becoming an ambassador, even though there were no black women ambassadors representing the United States at that time. "He told me that it would not be easy; and, when he told me what was required, I agreed with him. By the time he finished, I realized it would take me twenty-five years to reach my goal." Perry was a college drop-out at the time, married, and the mother of four children. "It actually took me thirty [years], because he left out working for the government." There were several ways to become an ambassador, Perry explained. Because of family responsibilities, she was not able to go the usual route of pursuing a foreign service career. "Perhaps the easiest way is to be financially committed to a president's fundraising efforts. I chose instead what I call a parallel career. I had a lot of related assignments. I did a lot of things with different national and international organizations."

Perry was advised to take a degree in political science, another in languages or English, and yet another with an international focus, such as international law. She would have to work for a private firm in the United States, and then work for five years overseas. "I decided my focus would be international law and followed that strategy from beginning to end. My strategy was to set a long-term goal, and then be patient and follow through, knowing that I had only a limited time for each short-term goal at any level. There were times that I had to break myself away to go to the next level. It was hard to leave IBM, which was the private sector of my goal. They were very good to me. It was difficult to say, 'No, I have to leave now and do my doctorate.' My doctorate was an important part of the agenda. The levels had already been established in my mind by my advisor. He had said, 'Do this degree, do another degree, and do another degree, but rest in between, then determine where you want to go next.' He told me not to deprive myself of time with my children. I did not have what I would consider a relaxed program—but it was very deliberate."

I was curious about why Perry had chosen to ally herself with the Republican Party. "My mentor suggested that I choose a political party and be faithful to that party. I was a political neophyte; I had never voted. When I asked which party I should choose, he suggested that I choose the party that I could trust. Because most people I knew were Democrats, I decided to go to the Democrats. The mayor in my little town of Terre Haute was a Democrat, and he was running for governor. I told him that I could help him win the election if he gave me a job. He agreed to give me a job but wanted to send me to Indianapolis or to Gary, where most of the black people in the state lived. I told him that I paid taxes in Terre Haute and did not want to go to another city. He told me that he would think about it and get back to me. I then went to the opposition party and told them the same thing. They hired me. I became a Republican and have remained one for more than thirty years."

One of Perry's difficult choices involved returning to college to earn her doctorate. Her husband presented her with an ultimatum: marriage or her Ph.D. She chose to get the degree. It wasn't easy for her to cope with the challenges of graduate school on top of her responsibilities as a divorced single mother. "There is always something lost. There are things I could have done better. But I made a deliberate choice between what I could do for my family and what I could not do. That was difficult."

After her divorce and the completion of her doctorate at the University of Massachusetts at Amherst, Perry was offered a teaching position at Texas Southern University in Houston, Texas. A short time later, she began seeing a professor at the university. They had known each other years before in Indiana. "In fact, he was my first boyfriend at school. We had not seen each other for twenty-five years. When we met for the second time, his wife had recently died. Early on I let him know that I was going to be an ambassador. I told him that he should know about my dream before he thought about marriage. I had to fulfill my dream; I told him that our happiness depended on the reality of that dream. When he understood that this was more than a preoccupation with me, he asked me to marry him. He felt my program would not bother him—but of course it did."

By the time Perry reached her twenty-fifth year of following her program without achieving her goal, she began to question her strategy. And then while working at Texas Southern University, she realized that she did not yet have governmental experience. She took a leave of absence and moved to Washington, D.C., to accept an appointment as head of the Education Division at the Agency for International Development. "It was through my connection with George Bush, who is from Houston, that I got that position.

"During my four years in Washington, I was quite lonely. My husband and children had remained in Houston. He refused to move to Washington because of his work at TSU; but they came to visit occasionally." Perry returned home from work each night with no one to talk to. In her loneliness, she began to give up hope. "I was beginning to feel that I was wasting my time in Washington. I thought that it might be better that I quit and go home. One day I called Dr. Robert Terry at the university—he later became president of Texas Southern. Dr. Terry told me that the university had a position for me if I wanted to come home. Dr. Leonard Spearman, the president at the time, told me the same thing: 'Let us know when you want to return so we can assure you a position.'"

Perry was just beginning to make plans to return to Houston when she received a call from the White House. In fact, she says it was almost immediately after she talked to her colleagues at Texas Southern. The White House emissary told her that they had something in mind for her, but they didn't tell her what it was. After a wait of three months more, the White House called again. Perry was told that the ambassadorship they had in mind had been given to someone else. "They wanted to know how I felt about not being chosen. I explained that I was employed, that it was not as if I did not have a job. I planned to stay where I was. The caller responded, 'Oh, no—we think you would make a fine ambassador.' I put the phone down, danced around, screamed, and went back to the phone and said, 'You are kidding, aren't you?' I had almost given up."

When I asked Perry about her relationship with her diplomatic colleagues and staff, she replied that she fought against being seen as unusual, which was how people tended to view her. "When I was in Sierra Leone, my deputies were all male and mostly white. Some of my staff began to refer to me as Boss. I said to them, 'You will refer to me as

Ambassador.' They, of course, said that they did not mean anything. What they were trying to do is decrease the difference between us, to be less formal. I did not want familiarity. We could be friendly and we could converse on a certain level, but I wanted to be addressed as Ambassador."

Perry was highly respected by her colleagues. "Most African countries do not have enough money to place an ambassador in every country; so most of the ambassadors I worked with were from Europe or the Middle East. I was vice dean of the [diplomatic] corps in Sierra Leone. The senior member is always dean. He was cordial and very helpful. I was helpful to him also. My relationship with my African colleagues was also quite good. I saw them as equals, while the Europeans did not." Perry invited African diplomats to her receptions. Surprisingly, many of the other diplomats did not.

Having chosen a field that is almost exclusively white and male, Perry has, throughout her career, interacted more with men than with women. During her doctoral program, she was the only black as well as the only woman in her classes. Male students waffled between being supportive and holding themselves aloof from her. She feels now that their attitudes helped prepare her for the rigors of her job.

Although more women are becoming ambassadors, the number of black women ambassadors is still small. "Colleagues from other countries are usually men. Very few countries appoint female ambassadors. So you are always dealing with men. And when you are dealing with Africans—especially Muslims—they cannot understand a woman as ambassador. Once they realize that you are representing the United States, that calls for respect. Sometimes they call you 'Sir.'"

When Perry first arrived in Sierra Leone—a male-oriented, Muslim country—she found it necessary to frequently remind her contacts that she was the ambassador. Ministers' wives expected her to take their sides in domestic disputes. Although Perry was sympathetic to their movement toward independence, and would assist these women in their causes whenever possible, she was first and foremost a representative of the interests of the United States. It took more than a year before the people in Sierra Leone seemed to understand her position: The local women expected her solidarity in every situation. "I would say, 'Yes, I know what your problems are.'" In many cases Perry couldn't do much more without alienating their husbands.

Nonetheless, Perry frequently accepted speaking engagements in Sierra Leone and did what she could on those occasions to promote the interests of the local women and the cultural enlightenment of the men. At a lawyers' association meeting focused on the topic of women's rights, she gave a speech about wife beating, a topic she'd never heard addressed before in public in Sierra Leone. "Wife beating is prevalent in many of the African countries, just as it is in this country. I reminded them that it was a worldwide problem, not only in Sierra Leone; but just because a man pays a dowry for his wife does not give him the right to do whatever he wants with her. This issue is a great human rights issue. When I finished my speech, the president of the country told me that he learned something that day. Wife beating was not a topic that Muslim women could speak about."

Although Perry achieved her goal of becoming a U.S. ambassador, she continues to be ambitious. She had to give up her ambassadorship when a Democratic president, Bill Clinton, was voted into the White House. At that point, she took up her academic career where she had left off, accepting a position at Texas Southern University. She does not plan to retire. "When I set my goal, I said that I wanted to be ambassador to Kenya. Although I have lived and worked in Kenya, I still would like to become its U.S. ambassador." Considering Perry's track record, it would not at all surprise me if she fulfills this aspiration as well.

PART IV

ESSENTIAL CONNECTIONS: FAMILY, CHURCH, SPIRITUALITY

Each of us has the right and the responsibility to assess the roads which lie ahead, and those over which we have traveled, and if the future road looms ominous or unpromising, and the road back uninviting, then we need to gather our resolve and, carrying only the necessary baggage, step off that road into another direction. If the new choice is also unpalatable, without embarrassment, we must be ready to change that as well.

—DR. MAYA ANGELOU,
Wouldn't Take Nothing for My Journey Now

CHAPTER 12

A BALANCING ACT: MARRIAGE, MOTHERHOOD, AND CAREER

"When I was young, I felt that I would not marry. I thought I would finish college and go back home and take care of my parents. Thirty would be a good age to marry. I did, however, have in mind the kind of man I wanted for a husband, almost to the color of his hair. I was down to the particulars of what his fingernails had to look like." —LYDIA PETTIS-PATTON

L YDIA PETTIS-PATTON talked with me about the difficulties faced by contemporary women balancing husband, family, and career. Despite her earlier resolve not to marry until she was a mature thirty, Pettis-Patton met and married her husband in college, when they were both twenty years old. "I envisioned in my mind all kinds of things I wanted my husband to be, and that is the man I picked to marry. Very early I determined that I would not marry a man who did not have an education. My husband is not only college educated, he is also a scholar, and has been a scholar all of his academic life. We . . . remained in college to get our degrees. Our first child, daughter Asha Jamila Louise, was born eight years later, in 1975. She was born in Bloomington, Indiana, while my husband worked on his doctoral dissertation in higher and special education." Their son, Ade Jabari, was born in 1979 in Petersburg, Virginia, where Pettis-Patton's husband had accepted a position in special education at Virginia State University.

Although family and home have never gotten in the way of Pettis-Patton's achieving her goals, she is family oriented. "I am not a very social person. My family is more important. I find fun in being in the quiet of my home, relaxed, not bothered by outside forces, not having to answer fifty questions by people at social functions. After work, I enjoy being reclusive. We go out to dinner as a family; we don't gather with friends much. My husband and I don't have that much time together, and the time that we do have, we try to spend it with our family."

Early in their careers, Pettis-Patton followed her husband as he advanced and moved professionally. But when they moved to Portsmouth, it was husband who followed wife. Pettis-Patton reports that her thoughts about marriage have changed tremendously from what her mother said it was all about. "When I was growing up, it was often the man who was better educated. Also, it was the man who decided where the family was to go when making a career change. However, I have always worked. When I was thirteen, I started working on weekends." When she married, Pettis-Patton continued to work, refraining from taking time off even when her children were born.

"We live in Portsmouth because this is where my job is. Portsmouth is one of the premier cities in Virginia. I had previously headed a parks department in a smaller town—Petersburg, Virginia. So when the position became available here, I said, 'I'm going to apply for it.' I just thought I would apply, not thinking that I would get it, since nearly everybody in recreation around the state and the country wanted the position."

The interview process narrowed the list of applicants down to twenty-two, all of whom were asked to write an essay. The list was then shortened to eight, and once again to four. When Pettis-Patton found herself still in the running at this point, her husband began asking her whether she shouldn't remove her application, since she wouldn't be able to make the move to Portsmouth anyway. "I was never concerned about his negative thoughts about the position," Pettis-Patton told me. "I kept going.

After they narrowed it down to four and then to two, I knew the job was mine if I wanted it."

When Pettis-Patton was chosen, her husband was faced with a difficult choice of his own. "He was a high-ranking administrator for the State of Virginia—Director of Teacher Education, responsible for the state certification of all teaching in higher, secondary, elementary, and vocational education. He gave up that job to accompany me and is currently a professor at William and Mary College. The family is very important to us both, and my husband did not let his ego get in the way of his coming with me on my career move."

Pettis-Patton learned at an early age from her parents to give back to the community some of what she has been given. In addition to their own children, she and her husband have helped a young woman who came from a family of fifteen children to achieve a college education. "We've helped Natalie since she was in the eighth grade. She recently graduated with honors from Hampton University . . . [None] of her family had ever gone to college. Recognizing her potential, we encouraged and supported her goals. In high school, she graduated fourth in a class of 540 students. At Hampton, she did even better. We had the honor of seeing Natalie graduate second in her class of 1,200."

ACHIEVING BALANCE IN MULTIPLE ROLES

In this day and age, most women want not only a career but a long-term committed relationship and the opportunity to bear and raise a family. These often conflicting desires present difficulties for women of every color in our society. I was interested in seeing how these difficulties have been met by the thirty-two women profiled here.

All but one of the women had dual careers—homemaking and outside work—at some point in their professional lives. All but nine of the women had children. At the time I did my research, ten of the women were currently divorced, five were widows, and one had never been married—in other words, half of these highly successful women are single.

Zelma Stennis had some comments to make about the breakup of the traditional family structure in the black community. "I think the most significant thing the black family has had since slavery has been each other. The social structure was in the home, the church, the black schools, and the black colleges. These structures, so important to the stability of the family, are slowly but surely deteriorating, causing a negative impact on the quality of life in our black community. Many of the homes are without fathers. Many single mothers on welfare have low self-esteem and feelings of accomplishment. Also, drugs and violence are taking their toll on many of our communities. We are dealing with educational systems that are devoid of human concerns, a system that lacks initiative toward helping to build confidence and other important learning qualities necessary for a productive life."

Vivian Bowser added, "It is important that young women who contemplate marriage seek a common ground in regard to their future. I see the need for some kind of balance between each person's dreams and goals, and the reality of work, marriage, and family.

"I have met many fine young women who are not interested in marriage. Some of them are interested in family, but not in marriage. When I first got over the shock and sadness, I could listen to them with compassion and empathy. Although I may not agree with their philosophy, I can understand their frustrations regarding the problems of [finding] eligible young men.

"When I was a young married woman, we believed in the sanctity of the home and the importance of the family unit, which included both mother and father. I am saddened by the direction this important institution is taking. Many seem comfortable with the status quo that has such a crippling effect. I'm not talking about whether it is sinful or not, or whether it is biblical or not. It is sad that we are not developing a strong value system under which our children can thrive and survive. No matter how comfortable the lifestyle is, if it is not a normal lifestyle, it will not have positive consequences, nor the quality of life that is expected in a normal man-woman relationship."

Among the women who chose to remain married, it was universally true that the men they lived with were both supportive of their careers and egalitarian in their outlook. Antoinette Handy told me that her husband was always better in the kitchen than she was. "The one aspect of marriage that does not appeal to me is cooking. Fortunately, my husband helped his mother in the kitchen when he was growing up. As the eldest of five brothers and sisters, it was his responsibility to help rear the younger children.

"My husband and I have a good relationship. At times I probably have been more out front than he. But I'm mindful of the male ego. Perhaps that is why I never continued in school to get a doctorate. I have received honorary doctorates, but I wanted him to be the official 'doctor in the house.'" Handy's husband is a retired political scientist and professor emeritus at Virginia State University, currently a visiting professor of political science at Jackson State University in Mississippi.

"The evening Mr. Washington proposed to me," confided newspaperwoman Ruth Washington, "we were dining in a small restaurant on Central Avenue. I told him that there were three things I did not do: I did not cook and I did not wash or iron clothes. I promised him that I would help in every other way I could, except housework. My mother thought I was crazy; she had never heard of a woman who refused to cook, wash, and iron for her husband. You must remember, this was not the '80s— this was the '40s."

Pediatrician Brenda Bass is married to Edward Roper, a vice president of a brokerage firm. They have two children, a boy and a girl. "If you have a husband who supports you—and I have that kind of husband— the balancing isn't difficult. I think the real juggling act comes when a woman with a profession is the mother of young children. There are not enough hours in the day."

Even though children are the focus of her professional expertise, Bass was in for a lot of surprises when she became a mother. "I just had no idea. You work all day and all night, particularly when you're breastfeeding. You are up all night, and then you go to the office the next morning. And you try to figure it out in terms of balance. That is what my husband and I had to do. One solution was to share the work with other people. A housekeeper was hired, because I could not do everything; she took over a lot of the responsibilities; but on the weekends, it's my husband and me. As in most marriages, I still do more—like buying the groceries and clothes for the children. I can't remember the last time I did not have to think of anyone except myself. I guess those days are gone for a while."

NASA researcher Pat Cowings doesn't give a hoot about convention. When she decided to marry, she tied the knot with Bill Tiscano, a graduate student on her research team. Tiscano, who is white, is currently her coinvestigator; their desks at work sit side by side. Cowings reports that they were lab partners for nearly seven years before they married one day between experiments. "I was thirty-one. It was a convenient thing to do, and we didn't see any reason not to do it. Any objections my family or the universe may have had against a mixed marriage, to heck with that. I'll do what I want to do. I am very fortunate in my selection of a husband. When I allow myself to be vulnerable, and sometimes fear that 'Those guys may be right,' Bill reassures me that my work is important. He understands why I have to do this."

Cowings and her husband had planned to postpone having a family until the completion of one of their long-term experiments for the space shuttle. Everything changed on that fateful morning when the space shuttle Challenger blew up in mid-air. "You know, working for NASA, and being married to my coinvestigator, we wake up in the morning and go to bed at night doing . . . shuttle experiments. So when the Challenger accident happened, everything stopped. There was something of a baby boom around the agency during the interval that followed, including the birth of our son, who was born in 1987."

Getting her son Christopher into the childcare program at the research center was the first difficulty Cowings faced. Even though she signed up for childcare three months into her pregnancy, there was no space until Christopher was nine months old. Cowings and her husband readjusted their work schedules and hired someone to help out. "Bill worked from one in the afternoon until seven at night, and I worked from nine to three-thirty, so I would be home before the woman who cared for Christopher left. My husband and I passed each other like ships in the night."

When Cowings has to travel, her husband and son travel with her. Whenever they traveled to other NASA centers, they called ahead to have Christopher placed at the children's center there during their meetings. "I would have been absolutely lost without my husband sharing the rearing of our son. When Christopher was little, Bill fed and changed him as much as I did."

Iris Rideau spoke of her marriage to her second husband, whom she married when she was nineteen and the mother of a four-year-old girl. "I was able to stay at home and take care of my daughter. I only had the one child. I did not have children by my second marriage. In fact, I was kind of a child myself. So in the beginning, when my daughter was in school, I was active in PTA and in chauffeuring her and the kids in the neighborhood. Soon after my daughter entered junior high, I decided to return to work. That was the beginning of my career."

Rideau credits her husband with helping her achieve her long-term goals. "I was young and teachable when we married. I was also receptive to his suggestions. I appropriated more and more of my husband's business acuity. I admired and respected his abilities and personal qualities . . . My husband was my first mentor. He had all the qualities and drive that I admired. We are currently separated, but he taught me many things that pertain to business, and I was a good student. The problem in my marriage was that I eventually felt stymied. He continued to consider me primarily as wife and homemaker. It was hard for him to allow me to get out of the kitchen and let me be the person I wanted to be . . . After seventeen years together, we separated."

Rideau tells me that she enjoys being single—she likes the freedom to travel and come and go as she pleases, without having to be responsible to anyone. "That is what I need at this stage of my life. I am very comfortable with myself. I love beautiful clothes. I eat properly. I go to the gym several times a week. I walk on the beach. I do all the things that keep me healthy—physically, emotionally, and spiritually." She and her daughter are very close, and she continues to have a loving relationship with her mother. "I have bought a place for my mother in Santa Ynez, California, near Michael Jackson's ranch. It is in a beautiful, wooded area . . . Also, I have a beautiful grandson whom I adore and look forward to spending more time with. His mother and I talk almost daily, and we're together on weekends. Although my husband and I are separated, we are the best of friends. What can I say? Life is beautiful."

Councilwoman Doris Topsy-Elvord was married from 1953 to 1968 to her children's father, then became a single mother. "I didn't want my children to have a stepfather, and they did not need one, so I did not remarry until 1982, when they were older. My new husband Ralph and I met through our jobs. I was a probation oficer and he was a baker and head cook at the L.A. County Probation Department. We are now both retired. When we were both working, one of the directors kept talking about this great guy that I needed to meet who was highly intelligent, very supportive, and—though a lot of other women were looking at him—she thought he would be perfect for me. She was right—he is. He encouraged me more than anyone to run for city council. He made his assets available to me, his time, and his love and support. I am truly grateful to him for that. One of my sons passed away two years ago. I had great support from my husband and my other two sons during my time of pain."

Although she married, Dolores Ratcliffe and her husband, now-retired dean of engineering and computer science at California State University at Northridge, decided not to have children. "With or without children, my husband and I still have to manage time. We have to plan time together, based on our schedules. When you are married, you have to communicate. It's always helpful to have someone who is not threatened by what you do. My husband has been successful throughout his life. Our childhoods are similar—we both had parents who were strong and guided our lives. We appreciate our mutual successes... He wanted to be involved with a woman who did things. We complement each other. The fact that we help each other with mutual problems is a real plus for both of us."

For fashion industry executive Kaycee Hale, a widow with no children, striking a balance between the personal and the professional is always a goal. Although currently in a special relationship, the nature of her work has made it difficult to have both a fulfilled personal life and a thriving career. Last year she made more than forty trips to different venues in the United States, Canada, Europe, Asia, and South Africa. "That in itself causes relationship problems, especially when I look at my calendar, which is booked into next year."

Senator Diane Watson has remained single because developing a meaningful relationship takes more time than she has to give. "Marriage and career—especially a political career—can be integrated into one's life, but it seems easier for men than for women. A woman needs to marry and start a family before she runs for an elective office. Her chances for marriage get slimmer and slimmer as she gets more and more involved in the political process. There is little time for dating and romance. I recommend to any woman who is interested in politics to get a personal life first . . . I do not think that every woman has to marry, but it helps to round you out. I'm sorry I did not—well, I can't say that I'm sorry. I did have some choices. But I did not take the path toward marriage. I was and continue to be driven toward service. I have lots of energy and can work around the clock. Sometimes I work until one and two in the morning. Politics is what I chose, and I give my career, my constituents, and the community one hundred percent."

Like Pat Cowings, Mary Jane Hewitt is in a highly successful mixed marriage. Her husband, Edward Rubin, is a retired businessman who owned a human and economic resources development company. I asked if her marriage had altered her career goals. "When we first married, my husband's kids were grown, and I never had children. Before he retired, Edward did a lot of business in developing countries, so he was gone much of the time. I was married before and divorced for ten years; so I was quite independent. Edward was home one month and gone the next, so nothing changed except my residence. When he was home, we were together and I had a different life. When he left, I went back to my old life of involvement. So, having to alter my lifestyle was not a factor. The most important factor in our marriage is that he is probably my greatest fan and cheerleader. He is very supportive, and I would say very proud of my writings and what I have achieved."

Norma Sklarek commented, "I believe that a professional woman needs a partner who is understanding of her needs. The male ego sometimes is very delicate. It very often cannot deal with a wife who may be more successful than he. When I moved to Los Angeles, I met Rolf [German-American architect Rolf Sklarek], a wonderful, understanding person. Although he was a lot older than I, we were soon married and lived many happy years [together] until he died . . . I am now married to another wonderful man, an African American. Cornelius Welch is a physician; we were introduced through mutual friends. Both Rolf and Cornelius possessed secure egos, and were able to accept my success because of their own successes."

Sklarek does not believe that marriage hindered her career. A devoted mother, she tried to strike a balance between married life, motherhood, and architecture. "When my first husband and I were divorced, it was not easy to care for two children and work. I was blessed with good health, a lot of energy, and two aunts who took care of the boys while I worked." For three years, in addition to raising two boys and working forty hours a week, Sklarek taught two evenings a week at a community college in New York City. When her eldest son, Gregory, was diagnosed as dyslexic, Sklarek enrolled him in a special private school where Gregory made only minimal progress in his reading, even though the tuition ate up half her salary. Sklarek relocated her family to California, bought all the books she could find on phonetics, and spent twenty hours a weeks teaching Gregory to read. "Within two years, he was reading at his grade level. When I went to school to discuss Gregory's progress, I soon realized that the teacher seemed to resent my teaching Gregory at home. Parents aren't supposed to know how to teach their children."

In retrospect, she says, she's amazed that she was able to manage the competing demands of motherhood and career, but she's very glad that she persisted. Unlike many other professionals, whose work is by and large invisible, Sklarek can see monuments to her tenacity and vision all over the United States and all over the world. Her younger son, David, is a successful attorney. Gregory, the boy who couldn't read, had a thriving career in the building industry until it went into a slump, and he is now working in telephone technology.

Philanthropist Eileen Norton was working as a schoolteacher when she met Peter Norton, then a struggling computer programmer, on a blind date. In a *New Yorker* profile from January 30, 1995, David Owen describes the odd trajectory of Peter Norton's life from nerdy adolescent to art patron and software tycoon. According to the article, Norton is a shy, almost antisocial man. He lived as a Buddhist monk for several years before discovering his genius for computer software programming and marketing. Born to a middle-class white family in Washington state, Norton is open about having been aware from an early age of his preference for black women. He recalls that he was struck by two things in Eileen's personals ad: the fact that she was fluent in English, French, and Spanish, and the fact that she was black.

After the sale of Peter Norton Computing Inc. in 1990, the Nortons set up the Peter Norton Family Foundation to endow their giving and ensure the foundation's perpetuity. Unlike most family foundations, the Norton foundation is known for disbursing their funds with a minimum of hassle or red tape. David Owen wrote in his article, "In 1990, Norton sold out to Symantec, a larger company, for stock that turned out to be worth over three hundred million dollars. Norton and his wife devote the bulk of their energies to raising their two grade-school-age children, buying art, serving on the boards of philanthropic organizations, and giving money away."

WHITHER THOU GOEST, I WILL FOLLOW

As a man makes his way up the corporate ladder or otherwise progresses in his field, his wife and children have traditionally followed the geographical path of his progress, no matter how difficult it is for the wife and children to leave their home, their friends, and their schools. For the first time in history, as women are pursuing their careers, the shoe is on the other foot: Husbands find themselves faced with the choice of uprooting themselves or suffering the consequences of a long-distance marriage.

"There are more couples commuting now than ever," Harriet Michel told me. "When my husband and I did it nearly twenty years ago, it was so unusual that we were written up in the *New York Times* and other newspapers and magazines. In 1977, when I had an opportunity to go to Washington, D.C., to work as President Carter's director of CETA in the Labor Department, it meant splitting up my family. My husband, Yves, knew I wanted to go, but he had businesses here in New York that he could not leave. It was a difficult decision, but we decided that I should go to Washington. Ours was a commuting arrangement for five years. We bought a house in Washington and kept our home here in New York. Our kids were relatively young at that time, so my husband traveled to Washington every weekend to be with us."

When Terri Wright wanted to leave her administrative job in Connecticut, she heard that the state of Georgia was looking for someone to head its Women's Health Department. "I did not tell my fiancé that I planned to apply in Atlanta. A few weeks after I applied for the position . . . , I was notified that I was being considered and was asked to come for an interview. Two weeks later, Atlanta offered me the job."

The move from Connecticut to Atlanta was not a problem for Wright's fiancé, because he knew how important the new job would be for her. Although it took him six months to find a job, they both felt that the decision was the right one. When I asked if she would have left Connecticut without her fiancé, Wright replied with an unequivocal yes. "I did not go into public health for the money, although quality of life is important to me. I went into it for the fulfillment of purpose. In Connecticut I was stifled and was not achieving my potential. In fact I was being buried in an environment that I was not comfortable in. Although my fiancé was one of the few good things that happened to me in Connecticut, had I stayed I could not have been a good person for him, my son, nor for the people I worked with. He had not lived anywhere except Connecticut; but concern about our future together helped him decide to take the risk. Financially, it was a rocky beginning."

Cynthia Perry and her second husband had a combined family, with children from both their previous marriages. Near the time when she expected her appointment as ambassador to come through, all the children except her husband's youngest son had moved away from home. This made it easier for her to decide to leave her family and accept a job in Washington. "My husband and my children, who were older, remained in Houston; he refused to move to Washington because of his work at Texas Southern. They came to visit me occasionally." When Perry finally received her assignment to Sierra Leone, her husband took a leave of absence from his teaching position to accompany her. While there, he was able to work on setting up Sierra Leone's first American school.

Antoinette Handy's husband did not accompany her when she was hired to head the music division of the National Endowment for the Arts. "My husband and I have a good relationship and an interesting, unique marriage. Before our retirements, we lived in two utterly separate worlds. I lived in Washington, D.C., and he lived in Virginia. Although we lived in different towns, we shared each other's social life. I attended those events that were important to him, and he did the same for me. We talked by phone two or three times a week." Handy's husband, a political scientist and professor at Virginia State University, retired in 1992. He is now a visiting professor of political science at Jackson State University in Mississippi, where they moved after her retirement in 1993.

Perhaps what can be learned from the experiences of the women profiled here is that a loving relationship, respect, consideration, encouragement, and emotional support are the ingredients needed to make a successful marriage coexist side by side with a successful career.

CHAPTER 13

THE BLACK CHURCH
AND SPIRITUALITY

"I was in seminary in 1941 . . . Hardly anybody at that time ex-
pected a black woman to go to seminary. I studied under such
notable professors as Paul Tillich, Reinhold Niebuhr, Harry
Emerson Fosdyck, George Buttrick, Mary Ely Lyman, and Sophia
Lyons Fahs—all top theologians. It was a very rewarding time to
matriculate. I was the second black woman to graduate from
Union Theological Seminary."
—THE REVEREND DR. ELLA PEARSON MITCHELL

ELLA PEARSON MITCHELL was born on October 18, 1917, in a
Presbyterian parsonage in Charleston, South Carolina. She was
the third of four daughters born to the Rev. Joseph and Mrs. Jessie
Pearson. "My father was outnumbered in our family of eight females.
In addition to my sisters, there were my mother's mother, my father's
mother, and a female cousin whose mother died in childbirth. We all
lived in the parsonage that my father built on the back lot of the church."

The church, Olivet Presbyterian, was located in an all-white neighborhood but served the spiritual needs of the nearby black community.
"The black congregation was ministered by white ministers until my
father came. He pastored Olivet Presbyterian until he retired thirty-eight
years later. My mother was an active member of the church when they
met and eventually married. She continued to assist his ministry after

they married and had a family. When my father retired, my mother was among the few living members of his first congregation."

During her youth, most of Mitchell's social contacts were with families in the church. "Not only did we get the benefit of a positive religious experience, [but] the church offered a social experience as well. Many times the children of our congregation came to our home for activities. It was the center of most of the parties and celebrations, because we had a large backyard with lots of space for tables and chairs. We did many fun things together."

As a teenager, Mitchell began to involve herself more and more deeply in religious work. Her father allowed her to preach, and she conducted vespers for Presbyterian conferences. "During my teen years, I developed a close relationship with several churches in the community. When I was thirteen or fourteen, I worked in seven different churches. By the time I was fifteen, I played the organ at my father's church. When my organ teacher died, I played the organ at her funeral and replaced her at the Baptist church where she played. My Sundays were spent in one or more of these churches. For a time I played piano for two churches—the Episcopal church at twelve-thirty in the afternoon and the Methodist church at four-thirty. It seemed that I was always traveling from one church to another."

When Mitchell graduated from high school and entered Talladega College in Alabama, she wanted to attend seminary for graduate studies. But then one of her sisters left her teaching job to marry. Mitchell assumed her sister's position. "I taught English. At that time, teachers in Charleston could not teach after they married. That year was very exciting, because the home economics teacher was a classmate of mine in high school, and now we were back together again. The history teacher was also a classmate and had just returned from college. The social studies teacher had just graduated from Fisk University and was interested in music. We had one of the best glee clubs that ever sang at that school. I played piano for them."

Mitchell taught for a year, then left to become a Sunday School missionary in Sumter County, South Carolina. Encouraged to apply at

Union Theological Seminary, a highly regarded institution, she was accepted immediately. "I met my husband, the Rev. Dr. Henry H. Mitchell, at the seminary in 1944. When he asked me to marry him, he reminded me that we were working toward the same goals, so why not work together? That was fifty-one years ago. After graduation, we spent the first year of our marriage at the North Carolina College for Negroes, now North Carolina Central. Henry replaced the dean of chapel, who had gone on a sabbatical."

Mitchell found herself pregnant with their first child just as her husband was about to travel to Northern California to direct an American Baptist Missions program. Mitchell went to live with her husband's parents in Columbus, Ohio. Their son, Henry Junior, was born in 1945. "We had four children: our firstborn, our two daughters, and a son from Korea whom we adopted in 1956. When our family decided to have a fourth child, our son asked if we planned a boy. I replied that I did not think God ever told a mother what she was going to have. My son then said, 'Well, you better leave it alone. We can adopt what we want.' So we adopted a brother for him.

"Three of our children are still living, but our firstborn, Henry Junior, died at age twenty-six of leukemia. We believe that the disease resulted from our son's exposure to radiation at a cyclotron institute in California. When Henry Junior was in high school, he was in a solid-state physics research summer program. During his junior year, he received a science award to do research with the National Science Foundation.

"Our son died in 1972, and we moved to Rochester, New York, after living in California for more than twenty years. The year our son died, my husband developed an illness that could not be diagnosed. I believe that it was depression from the loss of our son. Because of his illness, he took a medical leave; and, while on leave, accepted a position as scholar-in-residence at the School of Theology at the Claremont Colleges, which gave him an opportunity to conduct research for his doctorate.

"One day while I helped my husband research a project, the registrar at Claremont told me that a black woman had never received a doctorate at their school of theology. She asked if I would be interested in being the first. I was, of course; but final registration for that semester was just a few days away. To apply they needed my records and other materials from Colgate Rochester Divinity School. We contacted the office of registration at Colgate on Tuesday and received my records on Thursday. Registration ended the next day, Friday. I was also told that one of the professors was retiring, and they needed somebody in the field to teach. I was able to get my doctorate on a fellowship. In 1974, after spending one year in residence and the second year writing my dissertation, I received my doctor of ministry. In 1973, one year before I received my doctorate, my husband received a Th.D. as a result of his lectures and his qualifying examinations."

Mitchell spent most of her time being a mother and working in a teaching ministry until the middle '70s, when she received her doctorate. That's when she began to think seriously about preaching. "There is a general perception that women are not welcome as ministers in the Baptist church. [This has] several reasons, the most important being the church's autonomy, which creates an independence enjoyed by few other denominations . . . For the most part, men have said that women were not called to the ministry. That is a presumption. Who does the calling? It is my feeling that God has been trying to break through for a long time. But because of certain biases and restrictions on women, men have fallen into the belief that women cannot be heads of churches. They lean more on what Paul said than on deeper scripture. Deborah was a judge in the Old Testament. King Josiah held Huldah in high esteem. He respected her opinions. He recognized her understanding and authority regarding Mosaic Law. Throughout the centuries, women have challenged the barriers of prejudice and bias. Some have broken through and succeeded in their quest."

In 1988, Mitchell and her husband began a ministry at the Interdenominational Theological Center in Atlanta. In addition, she preaches in churches throughout the country. Mitchell has served on the General Board of American Baptists, USA, and as president of its educational ministries board. She sits on dissertation committees at numerous theological colleges and has lectured at universities and schools of divinity throughout the nation.

Mitchell is the author of three books: *Those Preaching Women* (Volumes I and II) and *Not to Preach*. In 1989, at her 50th class reunion, Talladega College awarded her an honorary L.H.D. (doctor of humane letters) degree, and in 1984 she was honored as Distinguished Alumna, Union Theological Seminary, New York City.

A VITAL FORCE

From their earliest arrival in America, black people accepted Christianity as a vital force in their lives, encouraged by such organizations as the Society for the Propagation of the Gospel in Foreign Parts (SPG) and the Society of Friends (Quakers). The SPG evangelists told slaves and owners alike that baptism did not mean freedom on this earth—that baptized slaves must maintain their servile humility. The Quakers, on the other hand, felt it far more important to take a moral position on slavery than to simply bring Christianity to the slaves. They not only condemned slavery as an institution, but were against their members owning slaves.

After the Civil War, negative attitudes toward black attendance in white churches led blacks to establish their own independent churches. This also led to the emergence of many leaders in the black religious community. Thomas Paul is credited with establishing the first Negro Baptist church in 1805, which included the congregation of Free Negroes in Boston and Philadelphia. In 1816 Rev. Richard Allen founded and was the first bishop of the African Methodist Episcopal (AME) Church. In this century, during the '40s and '50s, such leaders as Congressman Adam Clayton Powell, a minister at the world-famous Abyssinian Baptist Church in Harlem, and Father Devine, a religious cult leader, had thousands of followers throughout the nation. There are many leaders who have uplifted the black community in the past thirty years, among them Dr. Martin Luther King, Jr., Rev. Ralph D. Abernathy, Rev. Jesse Jackson, Malcolm X, Cornel West, James Lawson, Jr., and Joseph Lowery. In 1966, Harold Robert Perry became the first African American to be elected a bishop in the Catholic church. In the 1980s, two black women made ecclesiastic history: Barbara Harris was elected suffragan bishop in the Lutheran Church, and Leontine T. C. Kelly was elected bishop in the United Methodist Church.

The daughter, sister, and wife of ministers, Leontine Kelly credits the men in her life with developing and helping to sustain the spiritual flame within her. Now retired, Bishop Kelly was born in Washington, D.C., to a family of eight children. Her father, a minister, and her mother, a housewife, both spent their childhoods in Louisiana. "My parents combined personal piety with social concerns. We children were nurtured and encouraged to enter fields where we could serve others. I believe that my family environment motivated me to seek a career in education and later toward service in the ministry."

Before her election to bishop in 1989, Kelly was a minister at Ashbury Church in Richmond, Virginia, and was in charge of evangelism nationwide for the United Methodist Church. Bishops are the highest-ranking clergy in the United Methodist Church.

Unlike Ella Mitchell, Kelly only received her call to the ministry in later life. "Although I married a minister, I had no intention of becoming one. However, when I received my own personal call, I did not resist." Having left college in her junior year to marry and have a family, Kelly later returned to complete her bachelor's degree and teach school. She chose to teach because the work hours were compatible with her children's schedules at school. Years later Kelly earned a master's degree in divinity.

As with many women of her generation, Kelly had learned to think of college as a place to meet a potential husband as well as a place of learning. When she became engaged in her junior year, her parents urged her to wait until graduation before she married. "I was too much in love to follow their advice. I felt that I could return to get my degree any time, and I did return after three children. When I returned to college, my oldest child was in high school and my youngest was in elementary school, so I had to become more organized and more disciplined. I studied between five and seven in the morning, before the children got up. I didn't want to give up the responsibility of my family, because I loved that, and I also loved being a minister's wife." Kelly adopted a fourth child after her other children were grown.

Being a caring, productive wife and mother was not enough to save Kelly's first marriage. "For the first time in my life I experienced failure. When it happened I thought my life was over. I did not think that I could overcome that awful crisis. I had been very much in love with my husband, and I had a lovely family. I did not want my family to fall apart. It was only because of my commitment to my children, and the love and support I received from members of my family and my faith, that I was able to cope and begin life anew."

Kelly experienced a long and intensive struggle before regaining her self-esteem and her faith in the sanctity of marriage. She believed that she would never marry again. And then, she told me, "I was blessed with a second chance. I met a wonderful man who was also a minister. My new husband encouraged me, helped enhance my self-confidence, and helped me reclaim my self-worth."

When she returned to the university for her master's degree, she thought that it would be in history, but her plans changed when her second husband suddenly died. Kelly decided to enter the seminary to study for her master's degree in divinity. "I was moved by other people's faith in me, and I responded to that faith. I had intended to continue teaching. Instead it was God's plan to use me in the church. He uses the most unlikely people in ways we cannot imagine. It is God's divine plan to open doors for those unlikely people to enter."

Kelly thoroughly enjoys preaching. "I knew that I was doing what I was called to do, and I was spreading God's word."

HOPE, FAITH, AND PROMISE

The church continues to be a focal point in the lives of the majority of black Americans, and especially black women. Charles S. Johnson wrote in 1934 (in *Shadow of the Plantation*) that their church is the one institution over which black people are able to exercise control. "The religious emotions of the people," according to Johnson, "demand some channel of formal expression and find it in the church." That is why the rash of church burnings in mid-'90s America is especially horrifying, in that they strike at the heart and soul of the black community.

A goodly number of the women I interviewed for this book grew up in spiritually oriented environments, and many credit their spirituality for their success. A child of a Methodist minister, Antoinette Handy says that it was her parents who gave her life its solid moral foundation. She believes that their spiritual grounding—which included love, morality, ethics, and education—was the basis for her future success and achievement. Zelma Stennis and Faye Washington, also the children of ministers, expressed similar feelings.

Publisher Ruth Washingtonn was among the most explicitly religious of the women I interviewed. Our entire conversation was peppered with her interjections of scripture and avowals of her faith. She saw her relationship with God as a healing, sustaining resource in her life. "I have the power to do all things through Christ, who strengthens me, and my spiritual power is in the temple within me and comes forth because of my openness for good." As we spoke, she often interrupted to tell me, "God talks, and I listen."

While many people believe that their success comes from being in the right place at the right time, Lydia Pettis-Patton does not believe in luck. "Luck is the result of hard work and opportunity. I'm a believer in God. I'm a very spiritual person who follows the directives that He has placed out there for me to follow. I do think that there are definitive paths that He has chosen for me. Some of us believe that the voices we hear in our subconscious are just voices, but I listen to my subconscious. It is my God's voice, and I'm always tuned in to that voice. By following His directives, I've been able to do all things I've wanted to do with my life."

Delores Ratcliffe, in contrast, had this to say: "I'm a firm believer in luck. I think it was Doug Williams, the football player, who said, 'The harder I work, the luckier I get.' The ability to succeed has a lot to do with hard work and preparation." Eileen Norton told me, "As far as religion is concerned, I grew up in a moral and ethical family environment . . . I don't go to church now, because I feel that spirituality is within. As far as my family's lives at present are concerned, our spirituality is one of giving and helping to make the world a better place. To help and care for others, that is what we are all about."

Susan Taylor spoke of the role played by spirituality in the early part of her career. "Because I had my daughter . . . , I came home every night. And because I was at home, I read books on spirituality and listened to tapes. Whenever I doubted myself, I found the books I needed. I knew the ministers I could go to for spiritual support. In the 1970s, I consciously began my spiritual journey, which helped me overcome daily problems. It gives me courage and faith. It is what keeps me grounded and lets me know that I'm not alone. It lets me know that I can achieve anything I put my mind to, if I am willing to persist and work hard."

When Taylor became editor-in-chief of *Essence,* her monthly editorial changed in focus as she began to write about her own spiritual journey and about spiritual health in general. Called "In the Spirit," these popular columns have been collected in two books: *In the Spirit: The Inspirational Writing of Susan L. Taylor* (1993) and *Lessons in Living* (1995).

For all of these women, whether or not they linked their spirituality with the Christian church, the fulfillment of their goals has meant much more than material or professional gains. Each of them heeded another call that came from deep inside them—a call to persist in the face of discouragement, disappointment, or seemingly insurmountable odds; a voice within that kept their gaze steady and their eyes focused on their dreams.

Aleta Carpenter put it beautifully. "Young people must believe in themselves, and know what they want. For those who are older, I would tell them to maximize the talents, skills, and abilities that we all possess. Everybody possesses something unique within themselves that must be given back to society. I believe that. If they would take a moment to make an assessment . . . 'What am I interested in? What am I good at?' Regardless of what [your] strength is, build on that strength. Build on those skills and talents; go out and give back to mankind what God has given you. In addition to having brains, we also have to have heart. That is what makes life worth living . . . What these experts are calling emotional intelligence, black people call soul—and we have always had soul."

BIBLIOGRAPHY

Angelou, M. *Wouldn't Take Nothing For My Journey Now.* New York: Random House, 1993.

Baurind, D. "Socialization and Instrumental Competence in Young Children." In W. W. Hartup, ed. *Research on Young Children.* Washington D.C., : National Association for the Education of Young Children, 1972.

Bethune, M.M. Address at Texas Southern University, June 1950. Paraphrased quote taken from *Life and Times of Frederick Douglass.* London: Collier-MacMillan LTD (1962): 508. Revised edition of 1892.

Coles, R. *Children of Crisis: A Study of Courage and Fear.* New York: Dell Publishing Co, 1968.

David, J., ed.. *Growing Up Black.* New York: Avon, 1992.

Ellison, R. from Gross, S.L. & Hardy, J.E., eds., *Images of the Negro in American Literature, 21.* Chicago & London: University of Chicago Press, 1966.

_____. *Black Families in White America* Andrew Billingley. New Jersey: Prentice-Hall, 1968, 3.

Greenfield, E. *Bubbles.* Washington, D.C.: Drum and Spear, 1972.

_____. *Rosa Parks.* New York: Crowell, 1973.

_____. *Nathaniel Talking.* New York: Black Butterfly, 1989.

Johnson, C.S. *Shadow of the Plantation.* Chicago: University of Chicago Press, 1934.

Johnson, J. E. *The Negro Problem.* New York: H. W. Wilson, 1921. An article by William Seneca Sutton in University of Texas Bulletin, No. 221: 24. March 1, 1912.

Lerner, G., ed. *Black Women in White America: A Documentary History.* New York: Vintage Books, NY.

_____. Langston Hughes' poem, "Mother to Son." In *Jim Crow and Jane Crow* by Pauli Murray, 593.

Little, L. *Children of Long Ago.* New York: Philomel Books, 1988.

Mitchell, E. P., ed. *Those Preaching Women vol.1.* Valleyforge: Judson Press, 1985.

_____. *Those Preaching Women vol. 2.* Valleyforge: Judson Press, 1985.

_____. *To Preach or Not to Preach.* Valleyforge: Judson Press, 1991.

Owen, D., *New Yorker* magazine article, January 30, 1995.

Pauli, H. *Her Name Was Sojourner Truth.* New York: Appleton, Century-Crofts, 1962.

Ratcliffe, D. *Women Entrepreneurs—Networking & Potato Pie.* Los Angeles: Corita Communications, Inc, 1987.

Taylor, S. L. *In the Spirit: The Inspirational Writings of Susan L. Taylor.* New York: Amistad, 1993

_____. *In the Living.* New York: Anchor Books, 1995.

Wood, P. H. *Black Majority.* New York: W. W. Norton and Company, Inc., 1974.

Wright, M. in *Black Women in White America: A Documentary History.* Gerda Lerner, ed. New York: Vintage Books.

INDEX

Conari Press, established in 1987, publishes books on topics ranging from spirituality and women's history to sexuality and personal growth. Our main goal is to publish quality books that will make a difference in people's lives—both how we feel about ourselves and how we relate to one another.

Our readers are our most important resource, and we value your input, suggestions, and ideas. We'd love to hear from you—after all, we are publishing books for you!

For a complete catalog or to get on our mailing list, please contact us at:

CONARI PRESS

2550 Ninth Street, Suite 101, Berkeley, California 94710
800-685-9595 • Fax 510-649-7190 • e-mail Conaripub@aol.com